This Coloring Book

Belongs To:

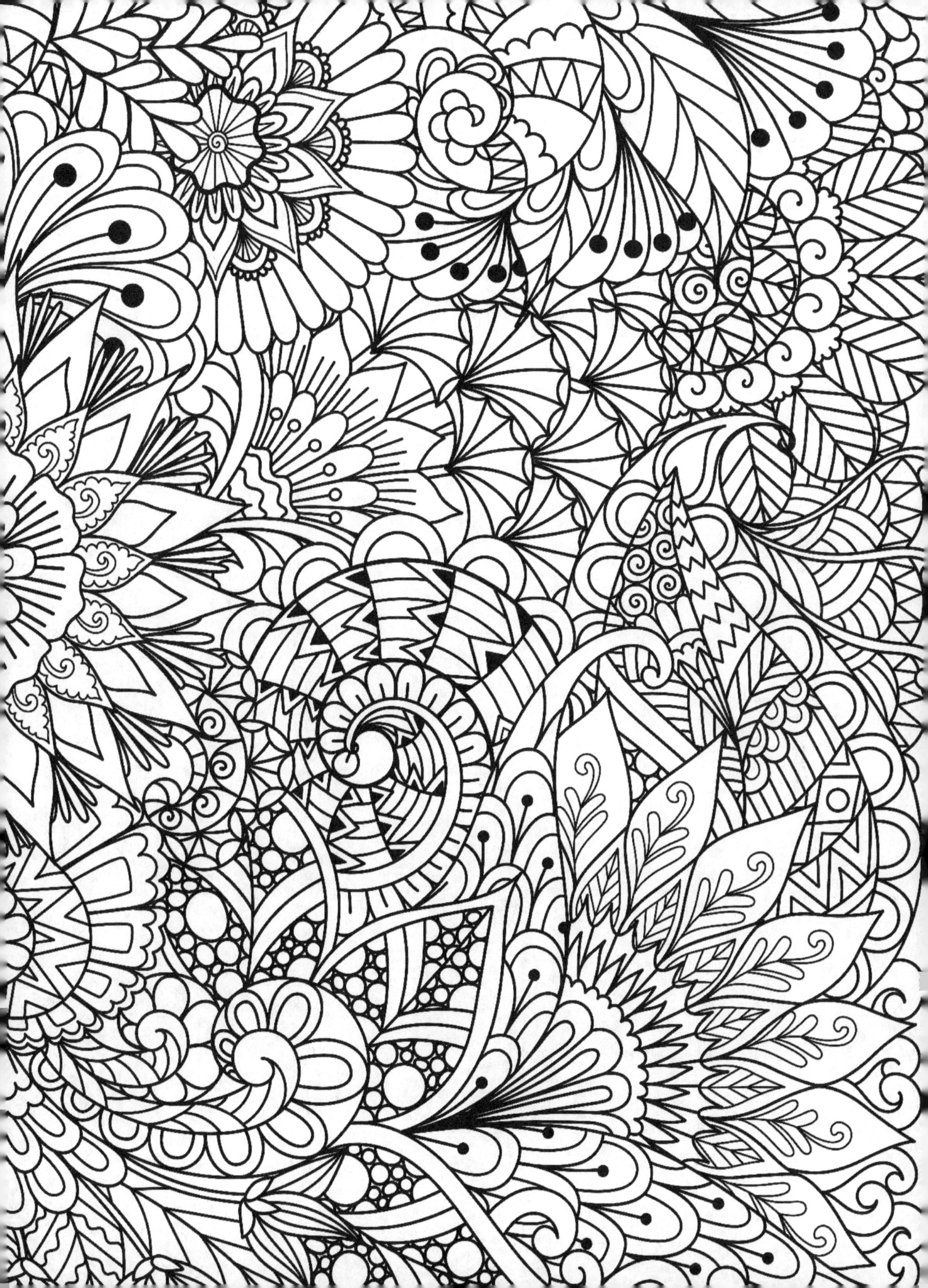

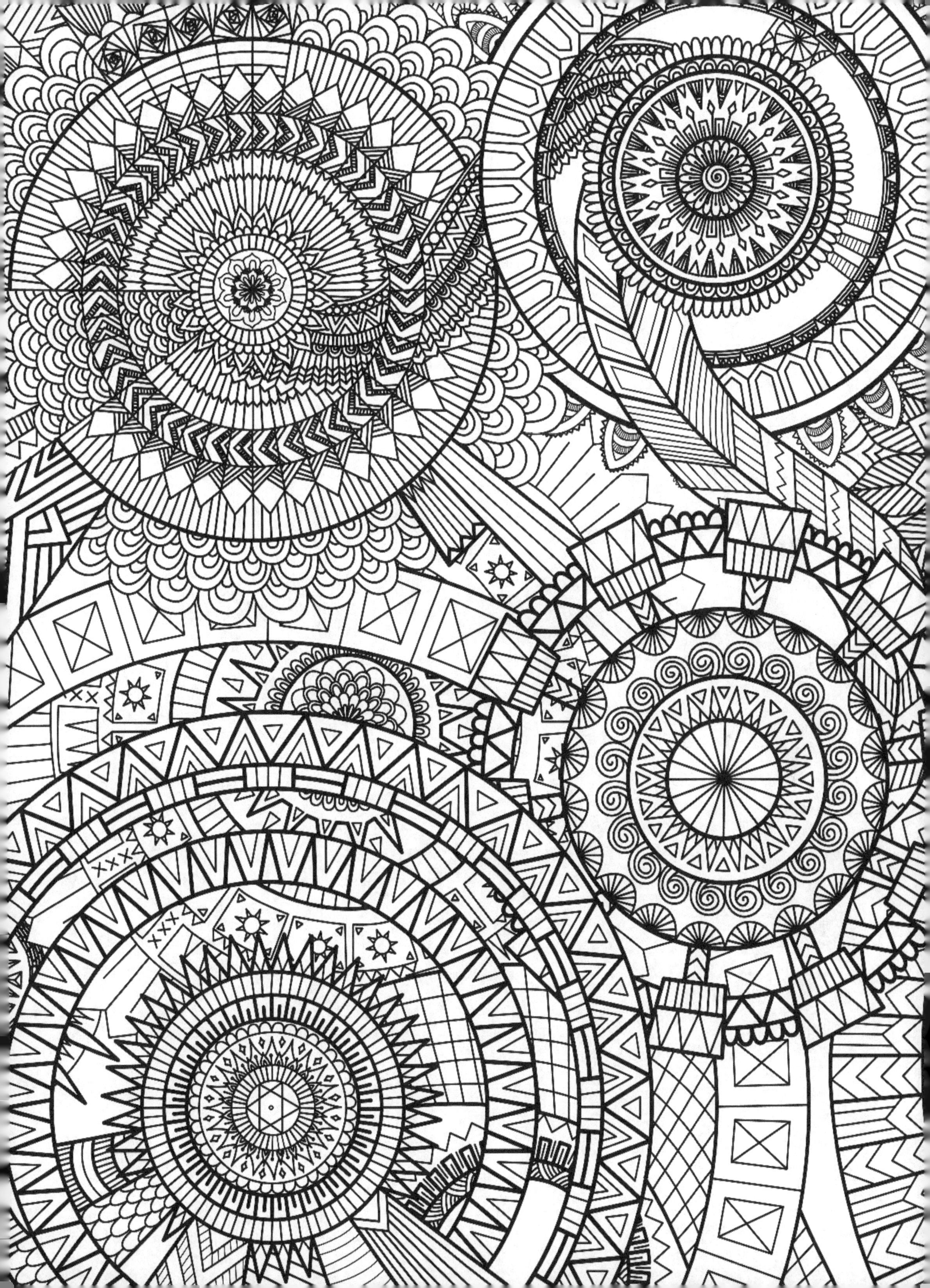

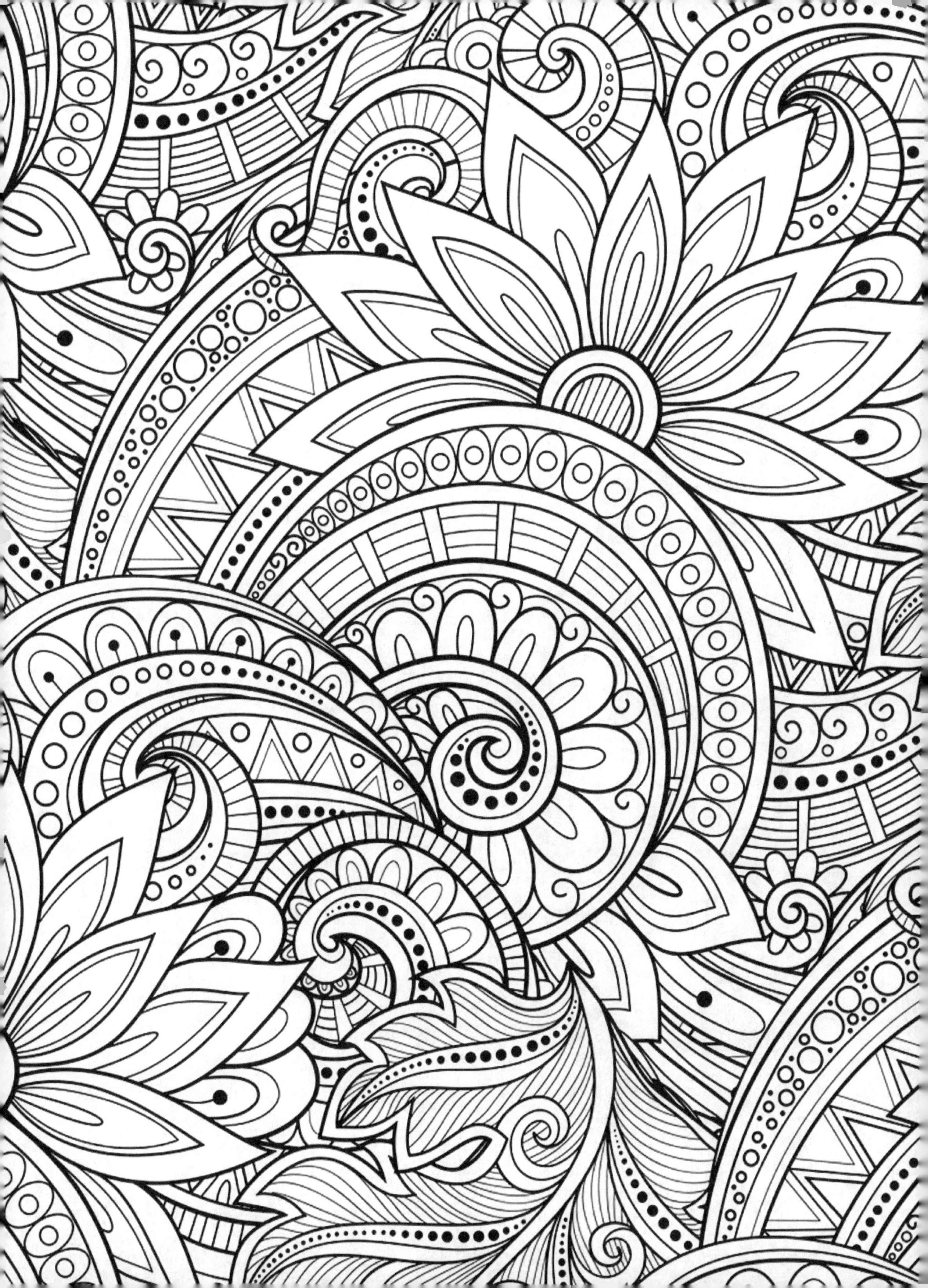

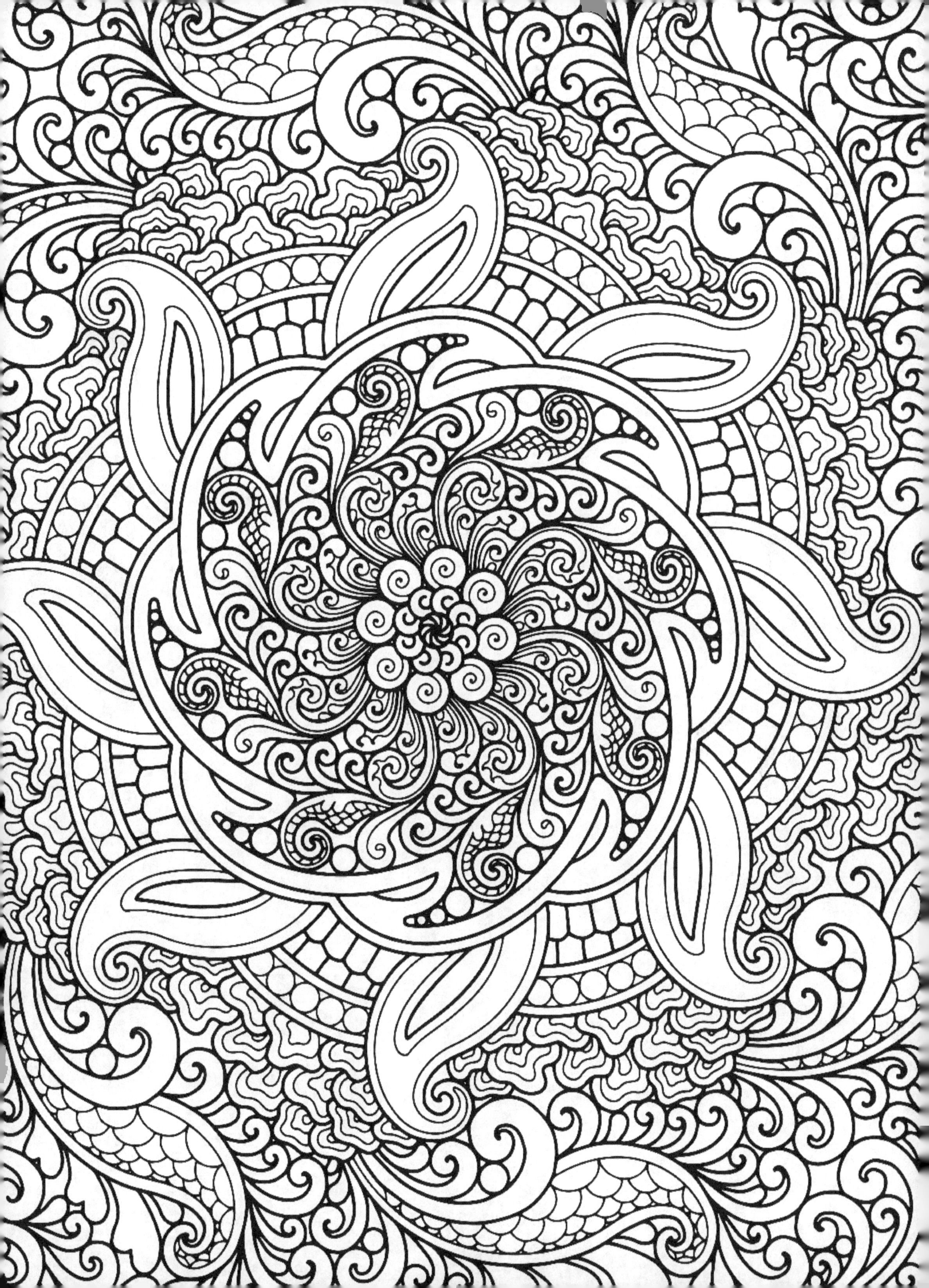

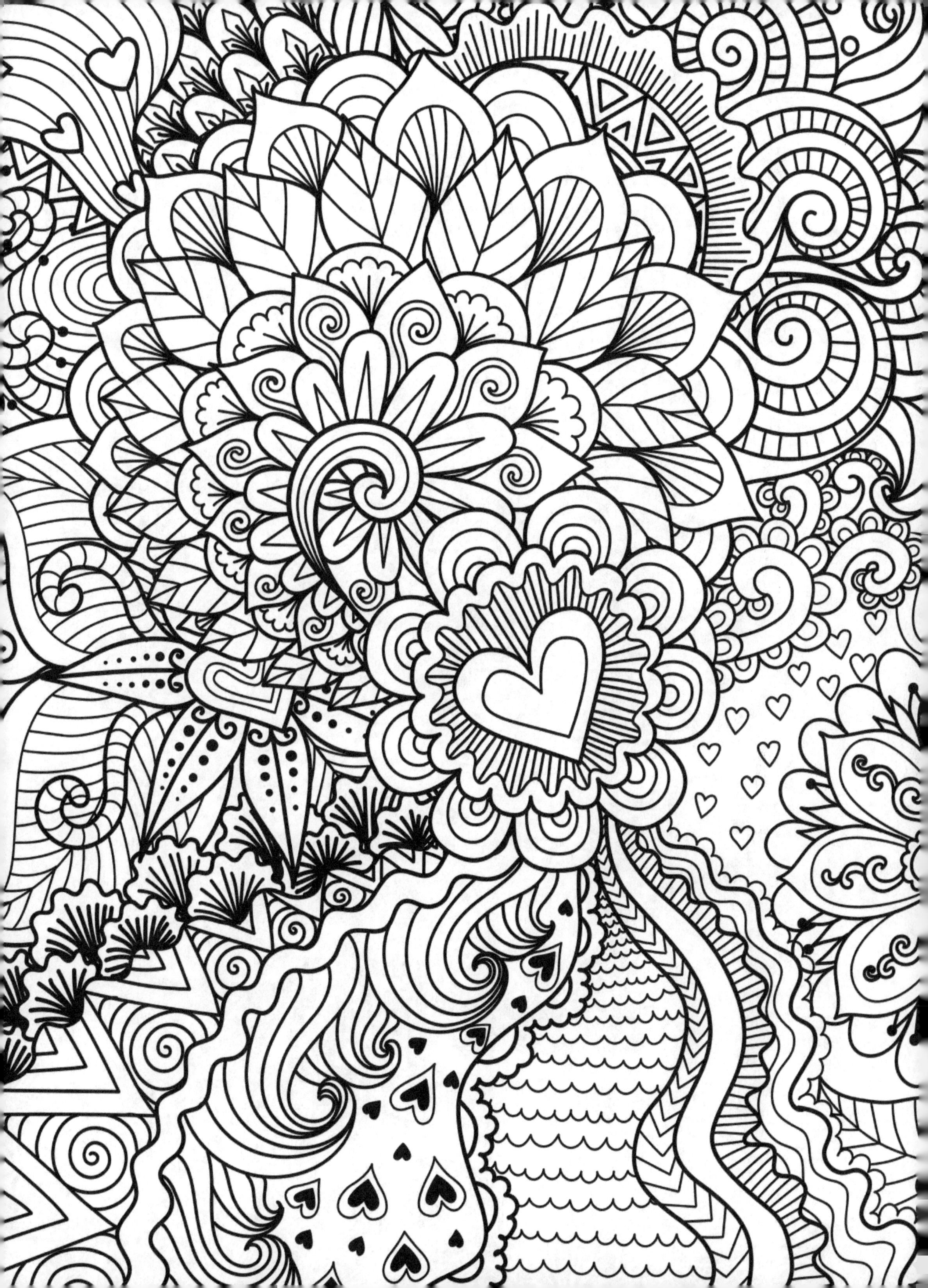

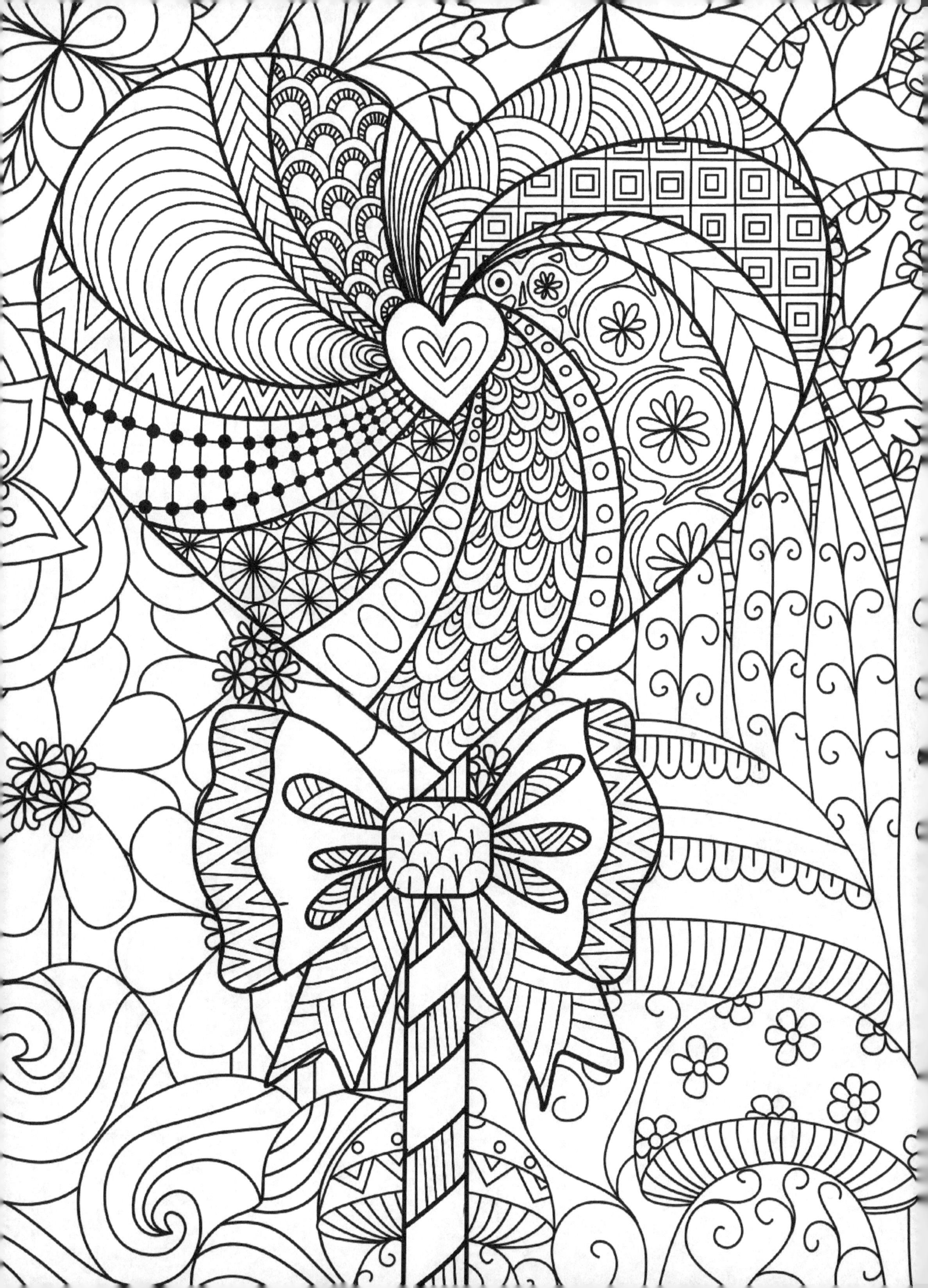

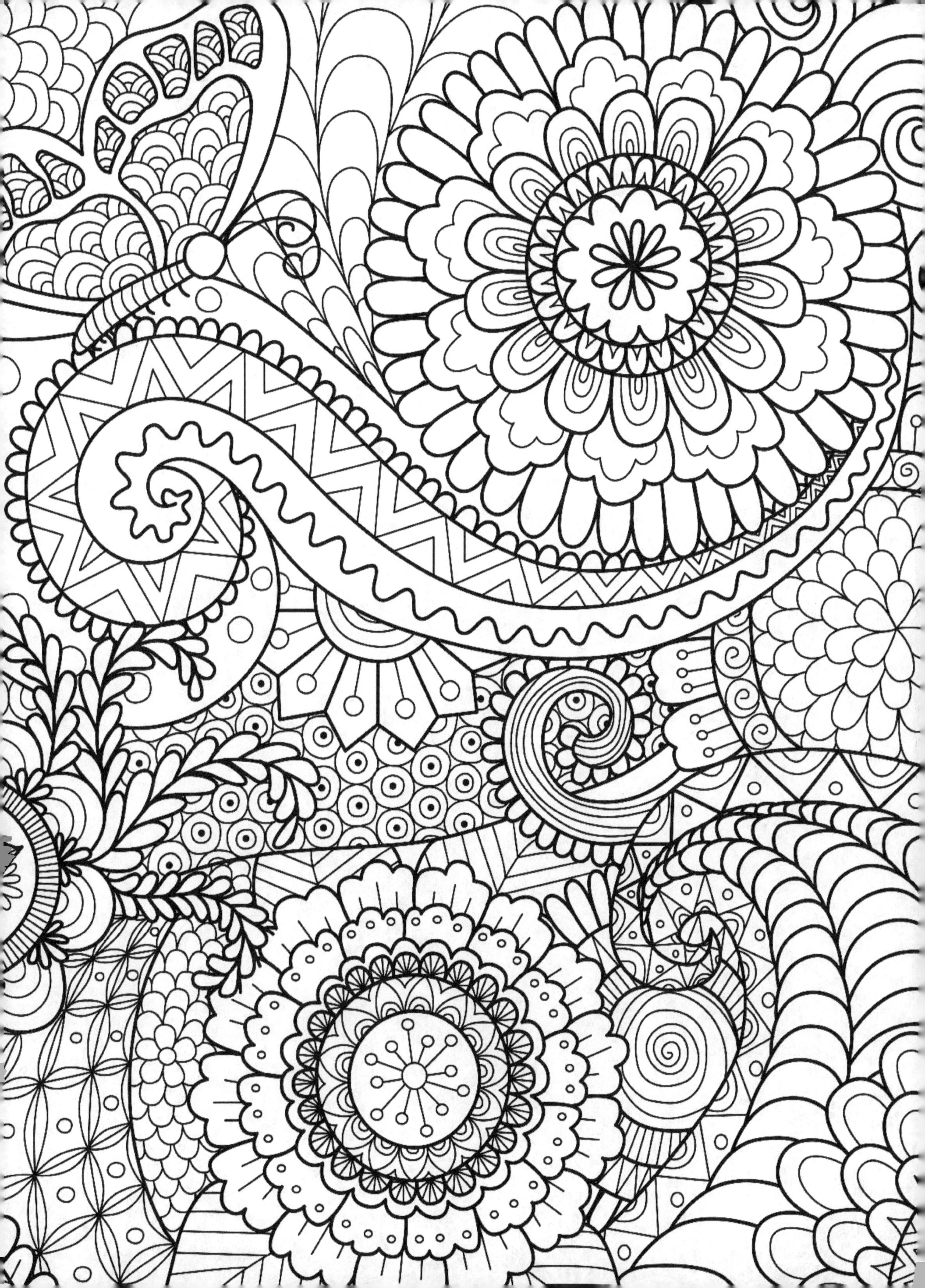

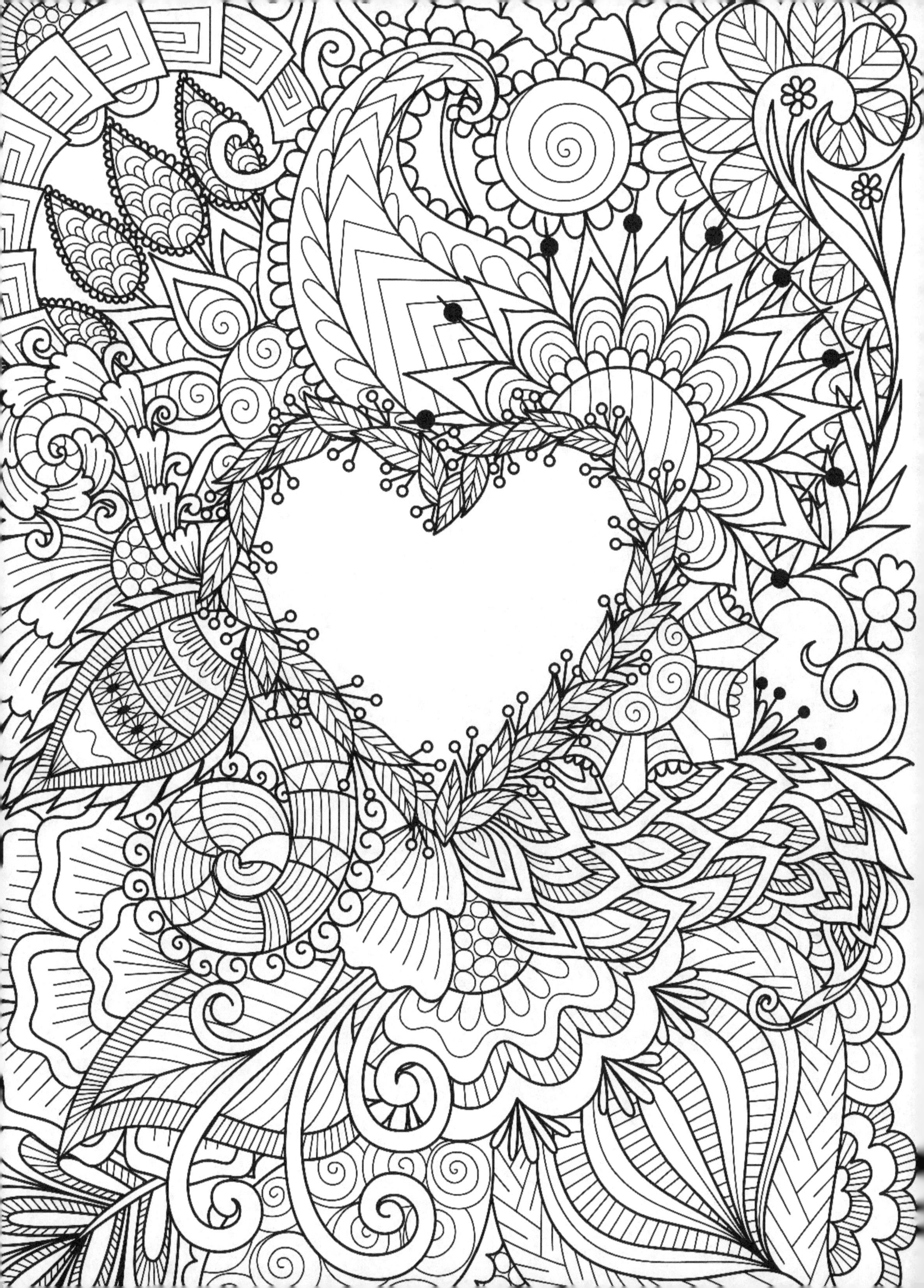

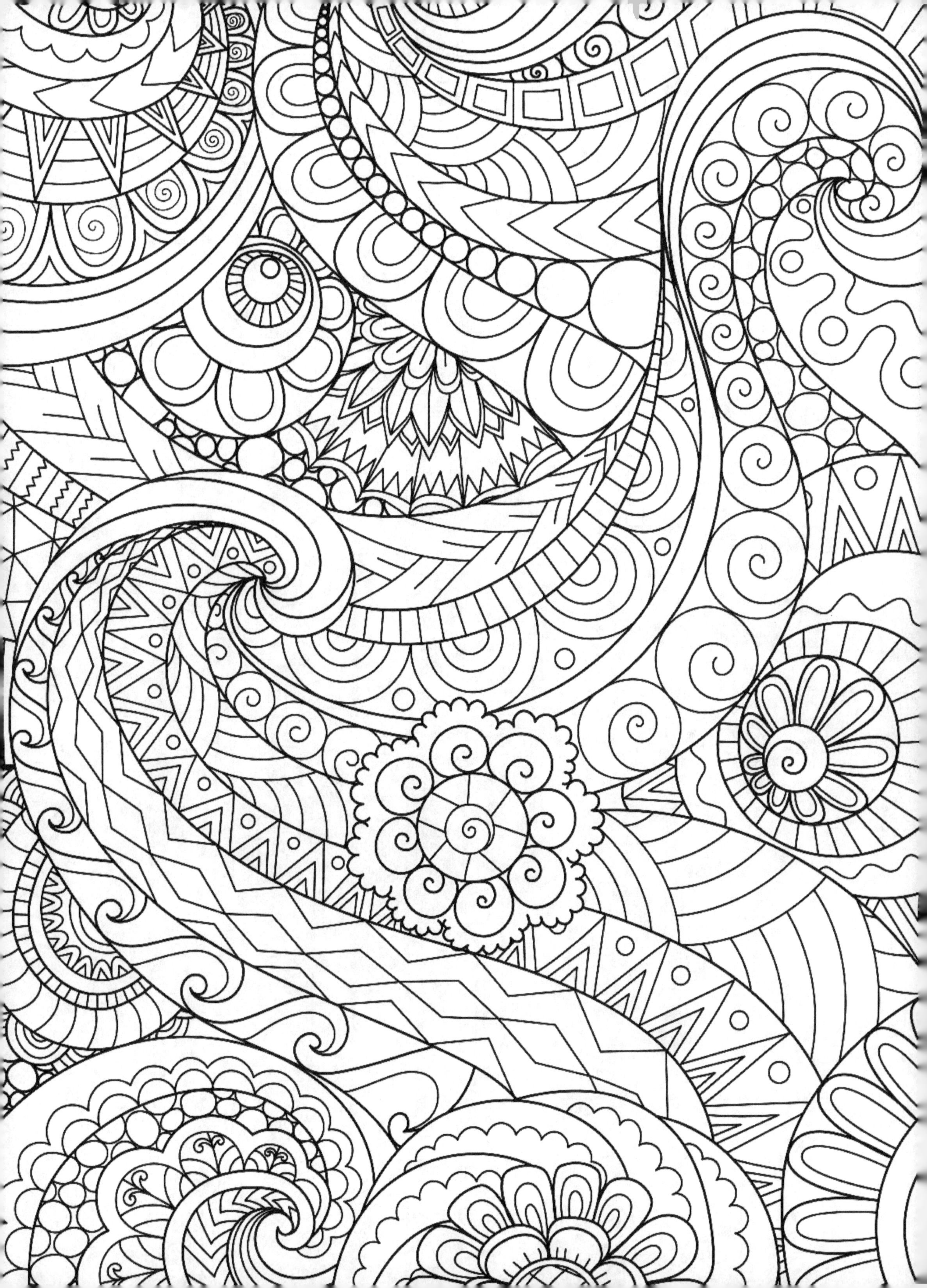

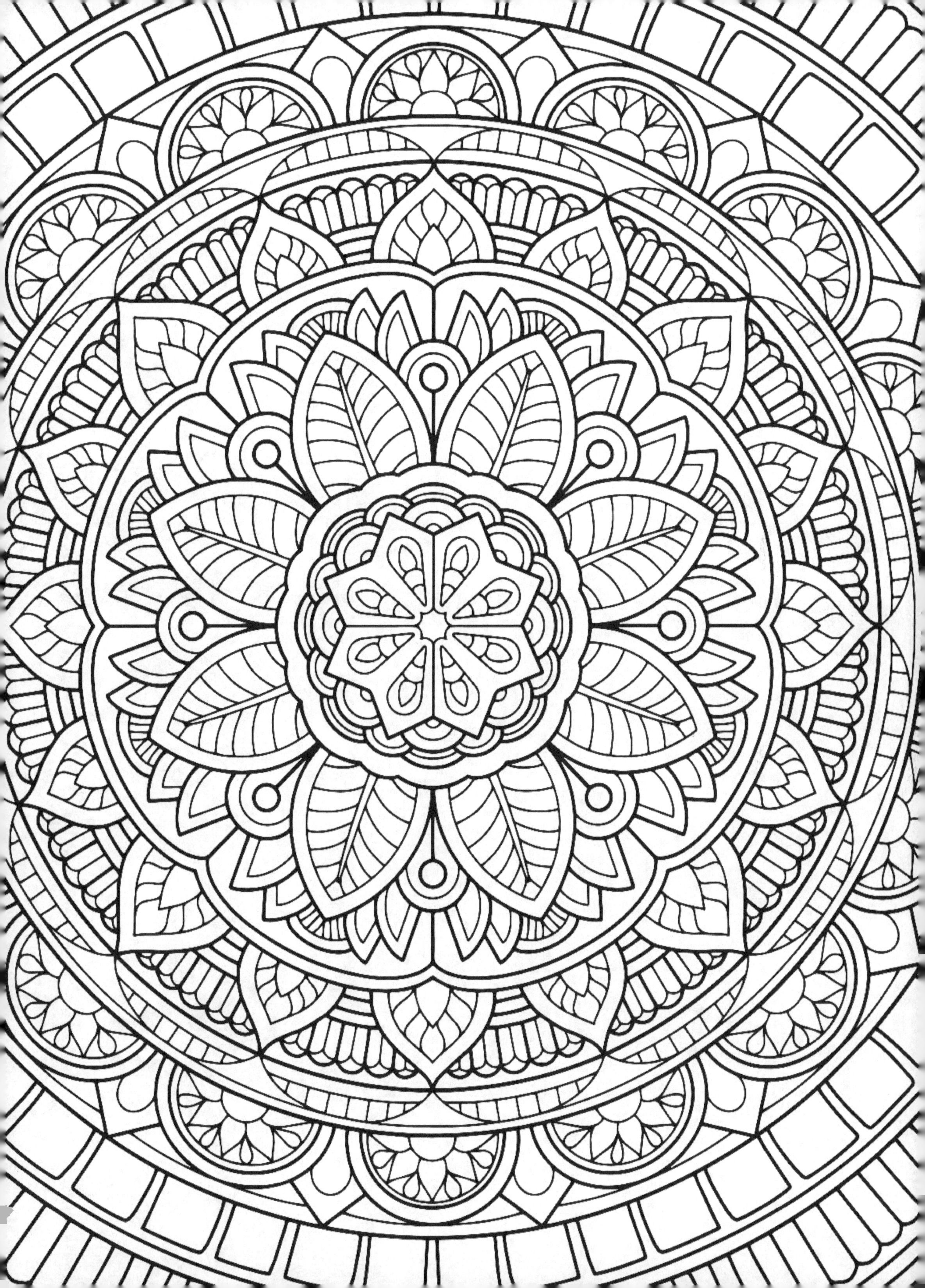

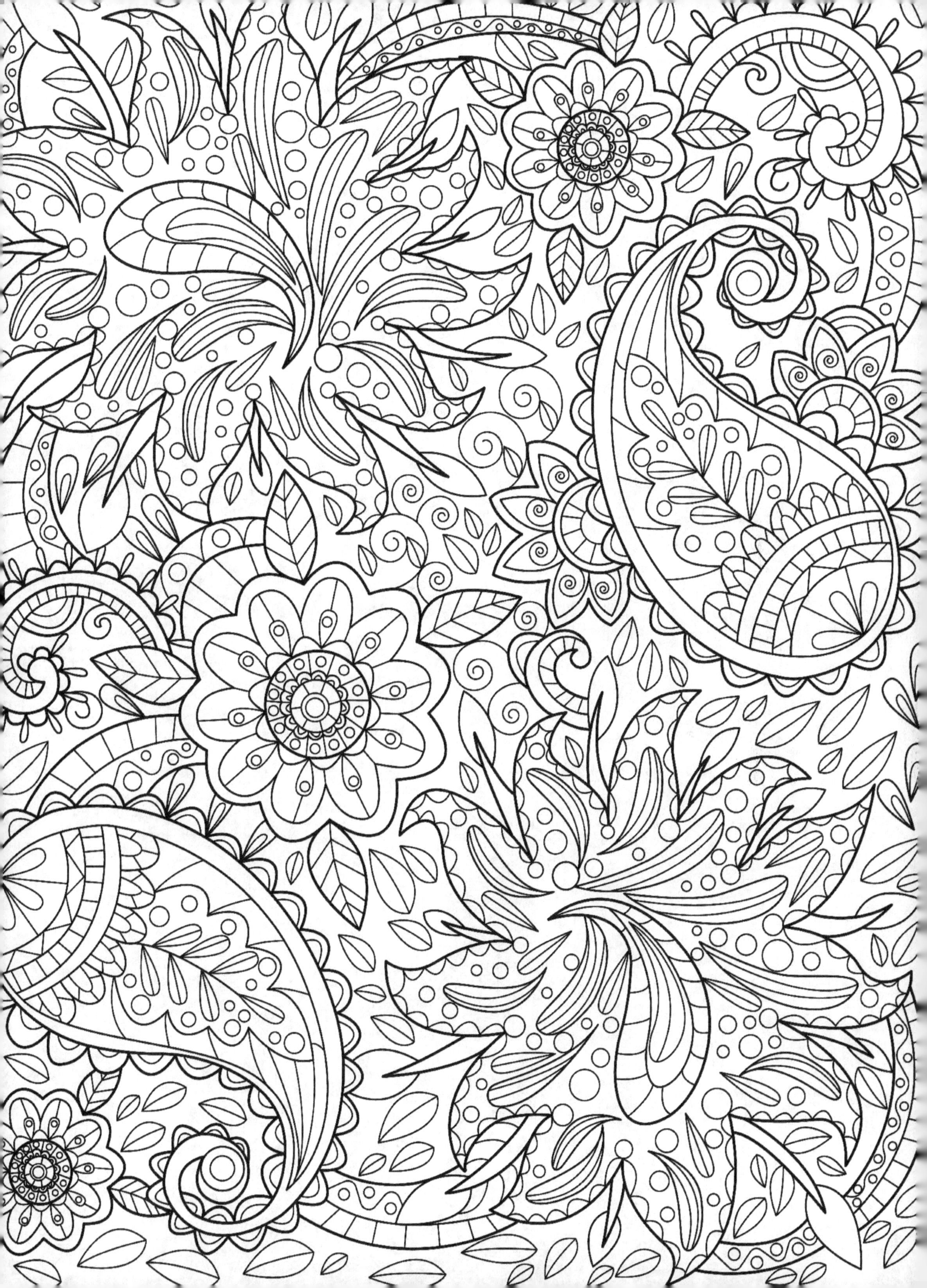

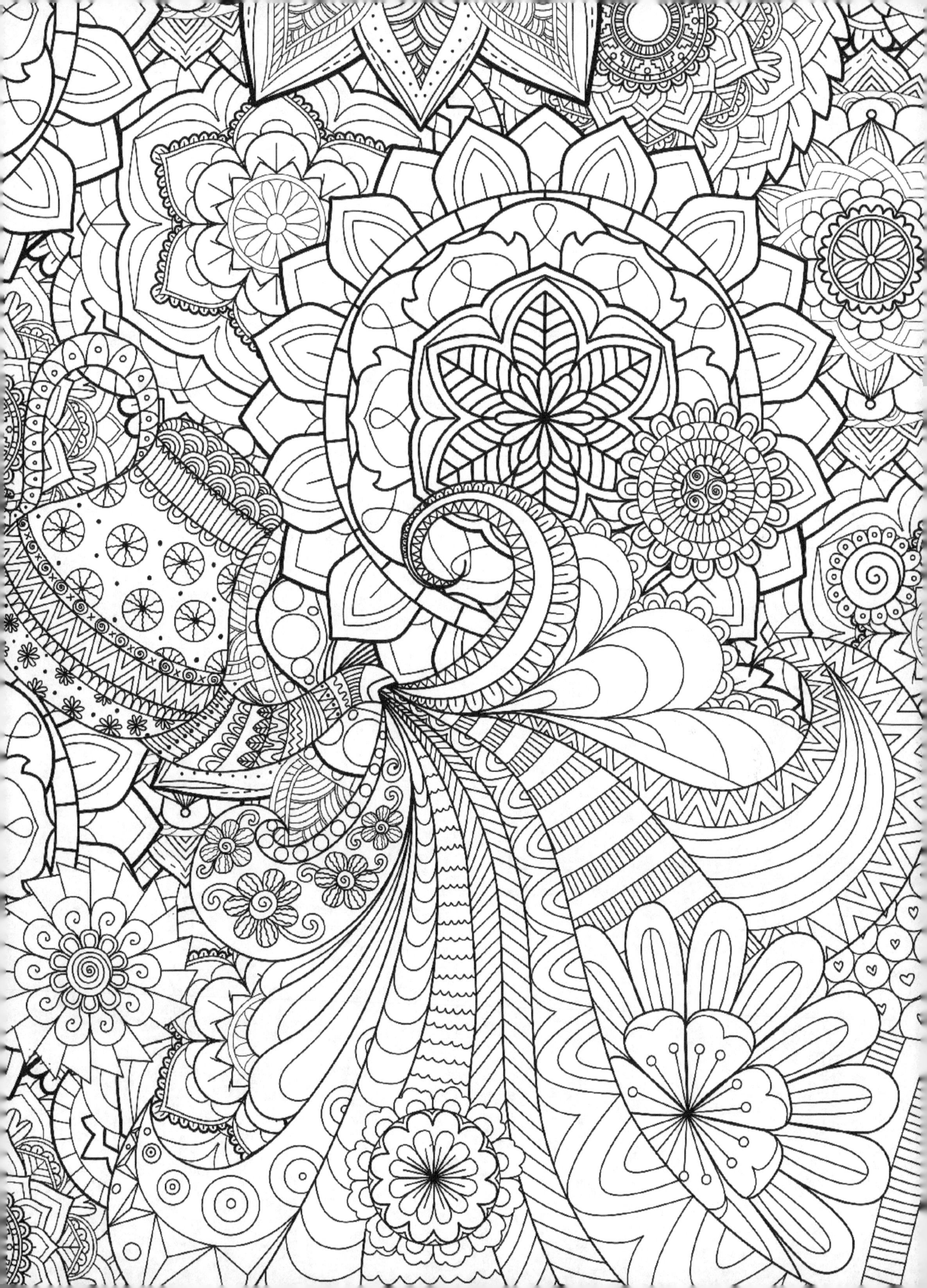

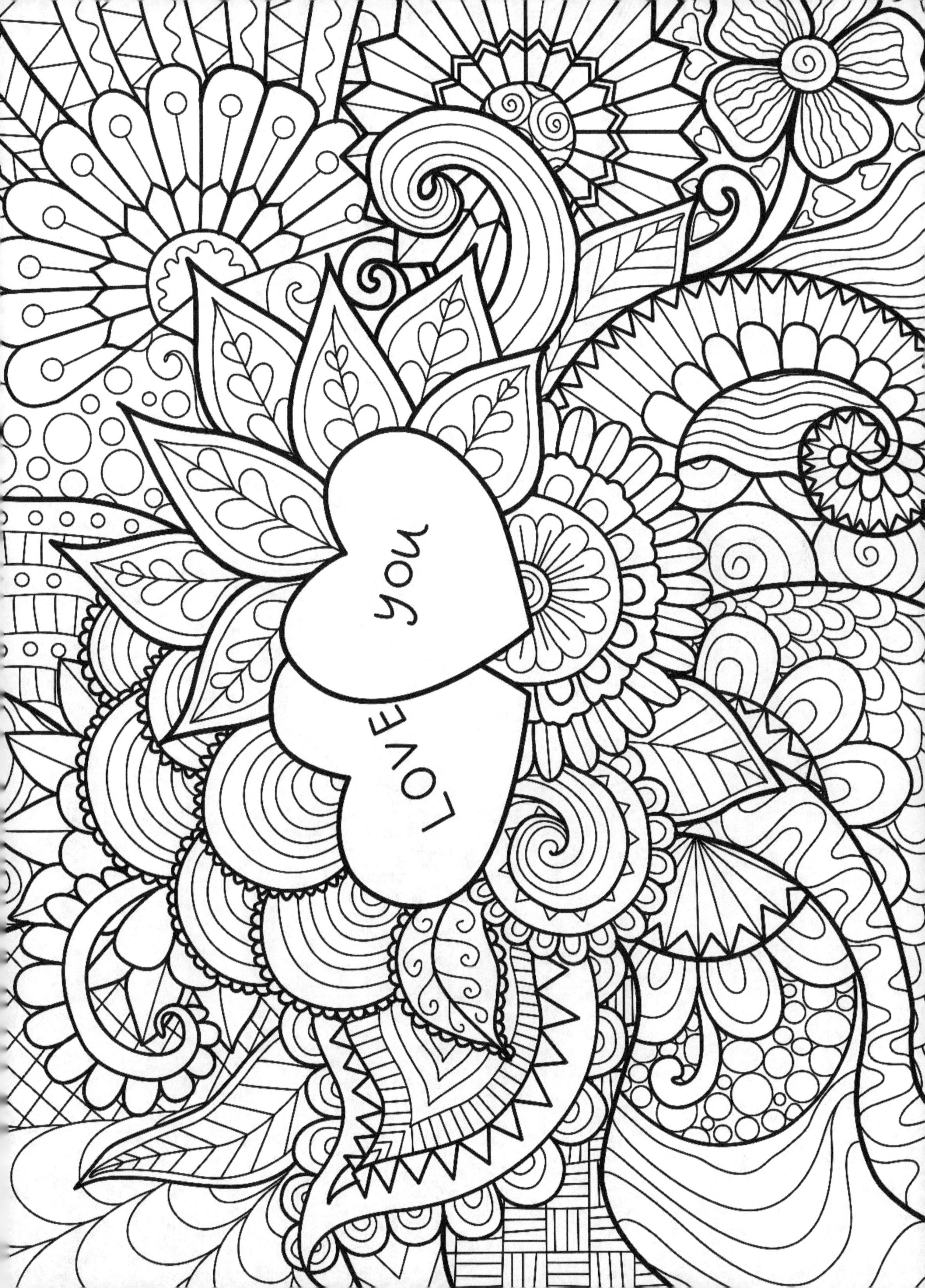

you
LOVE

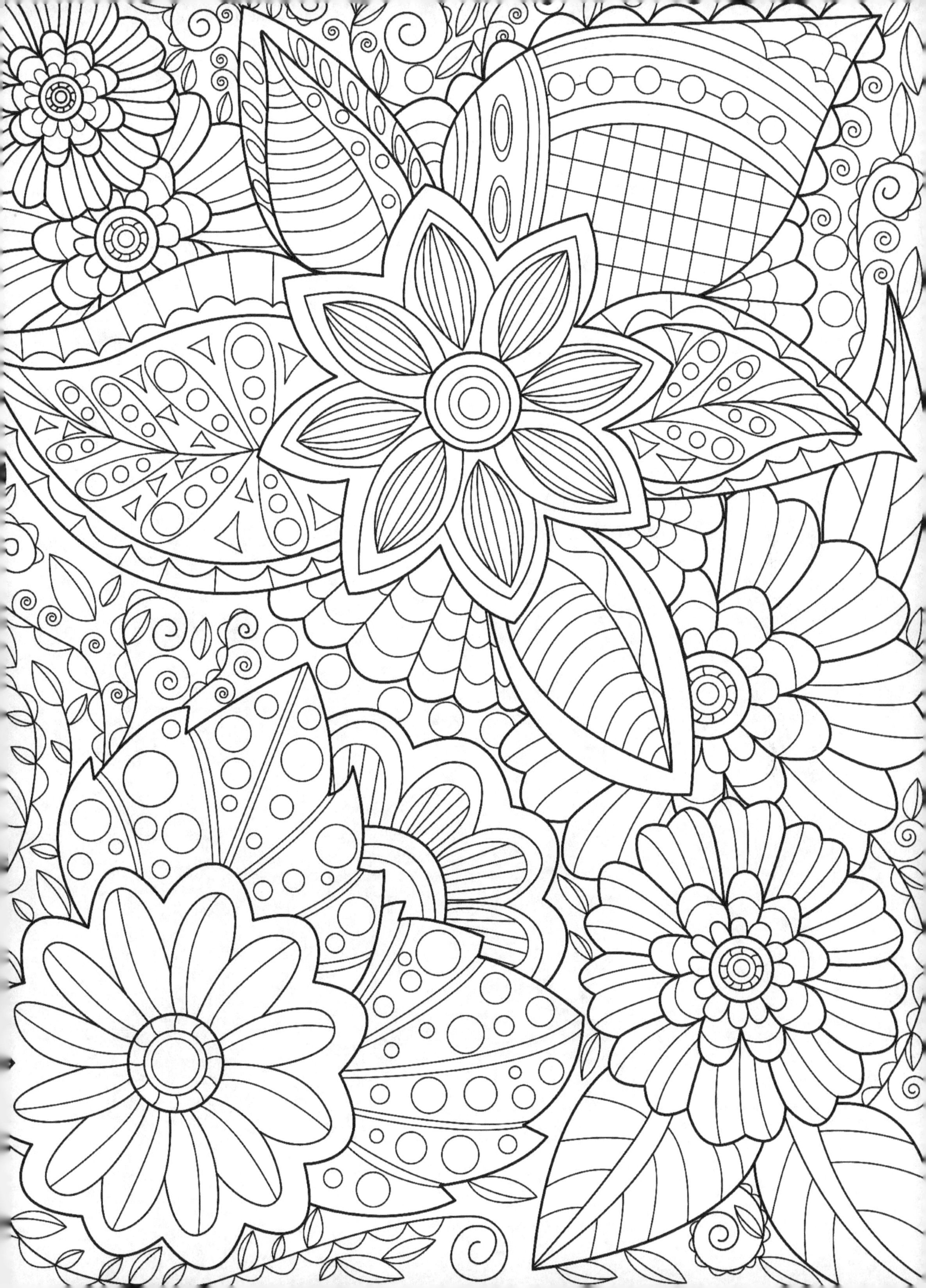

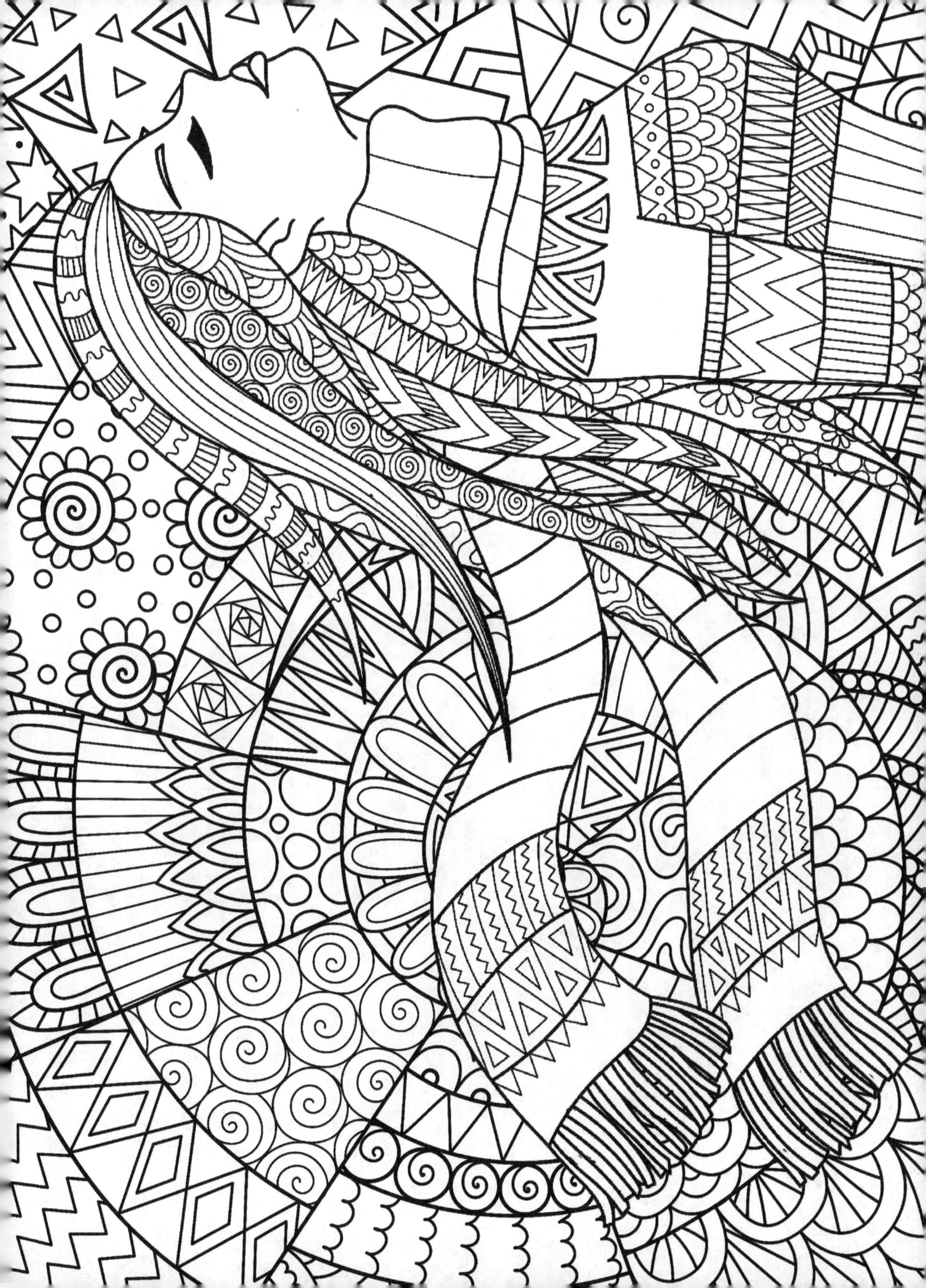

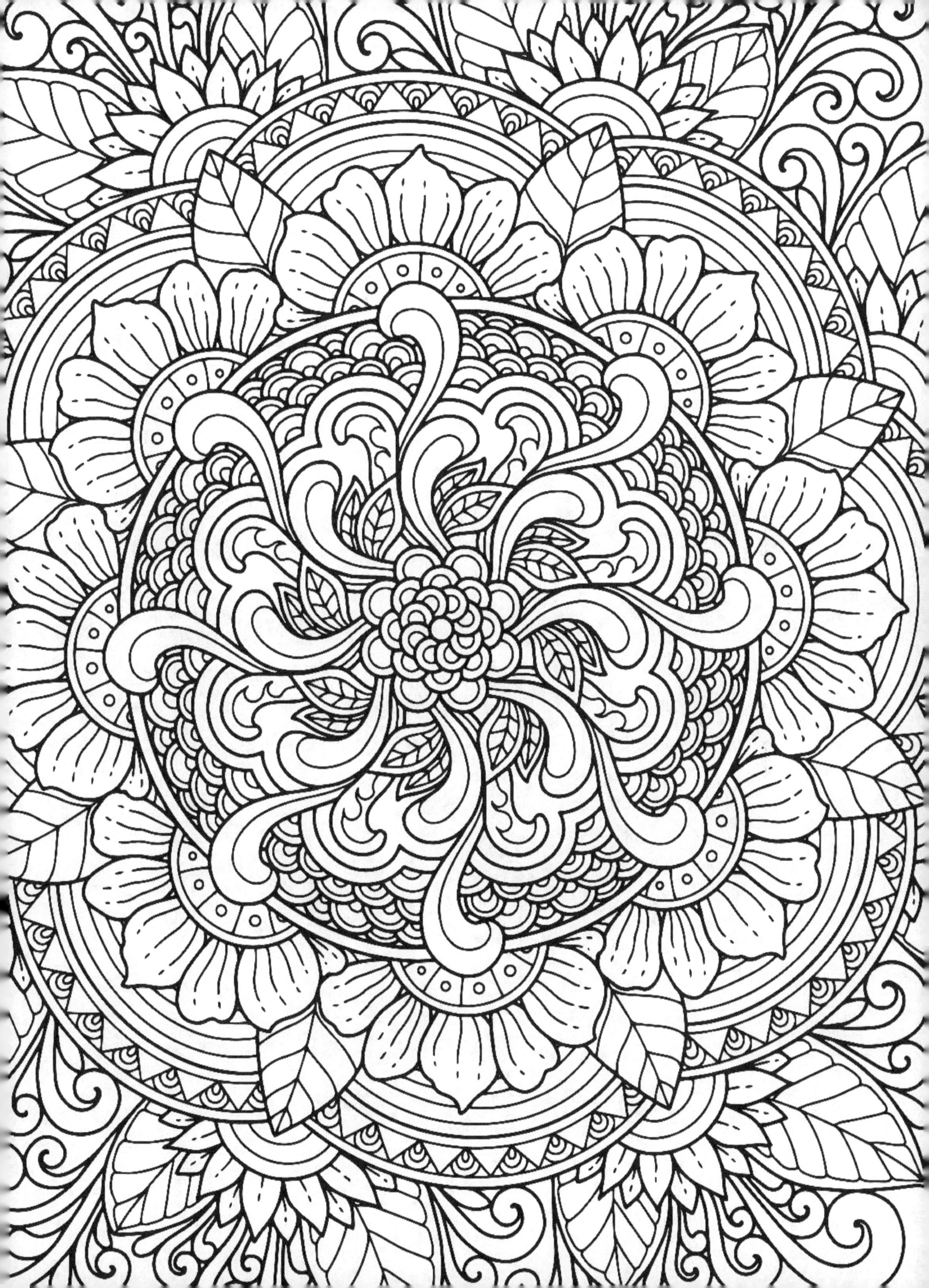

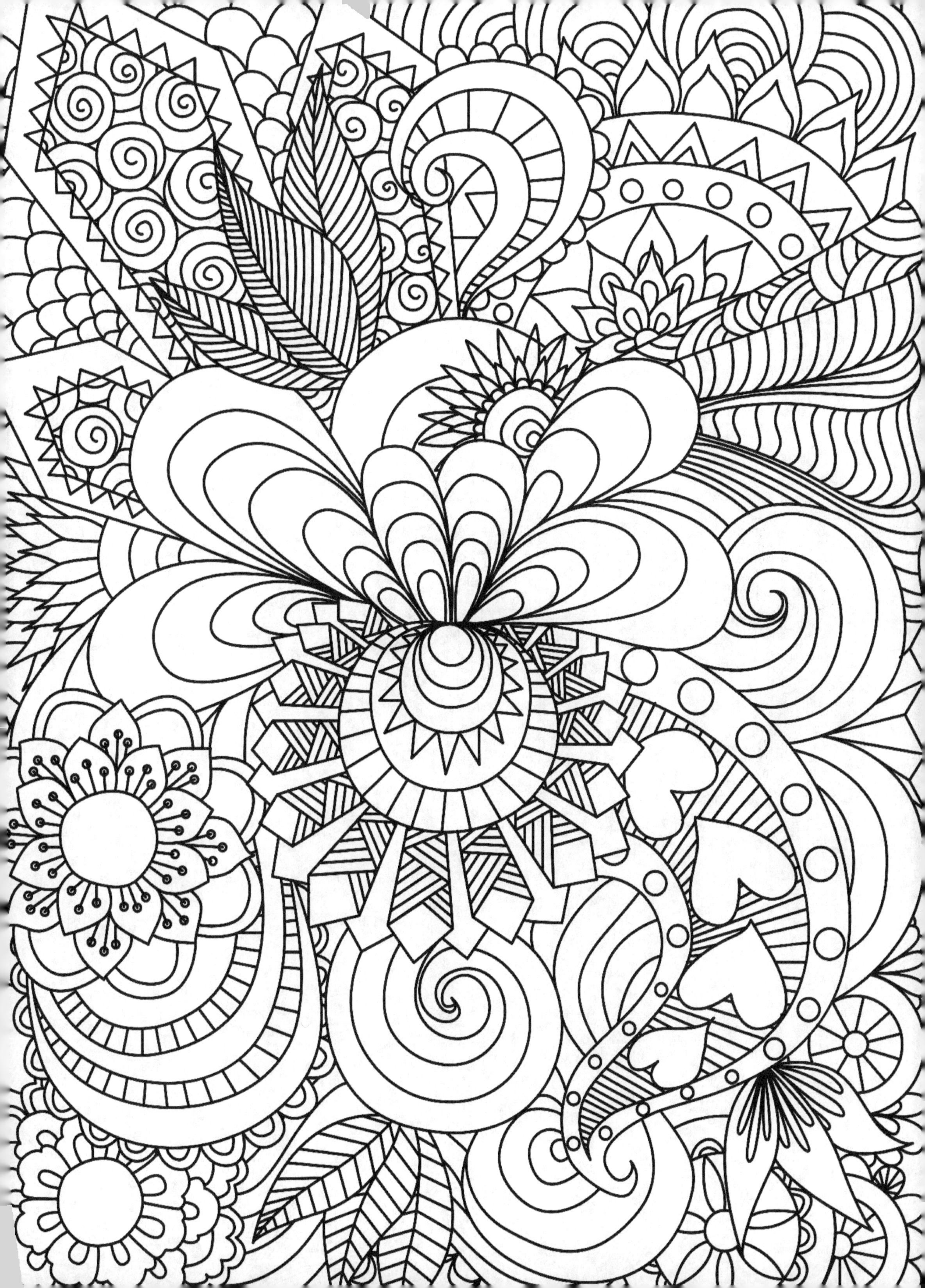

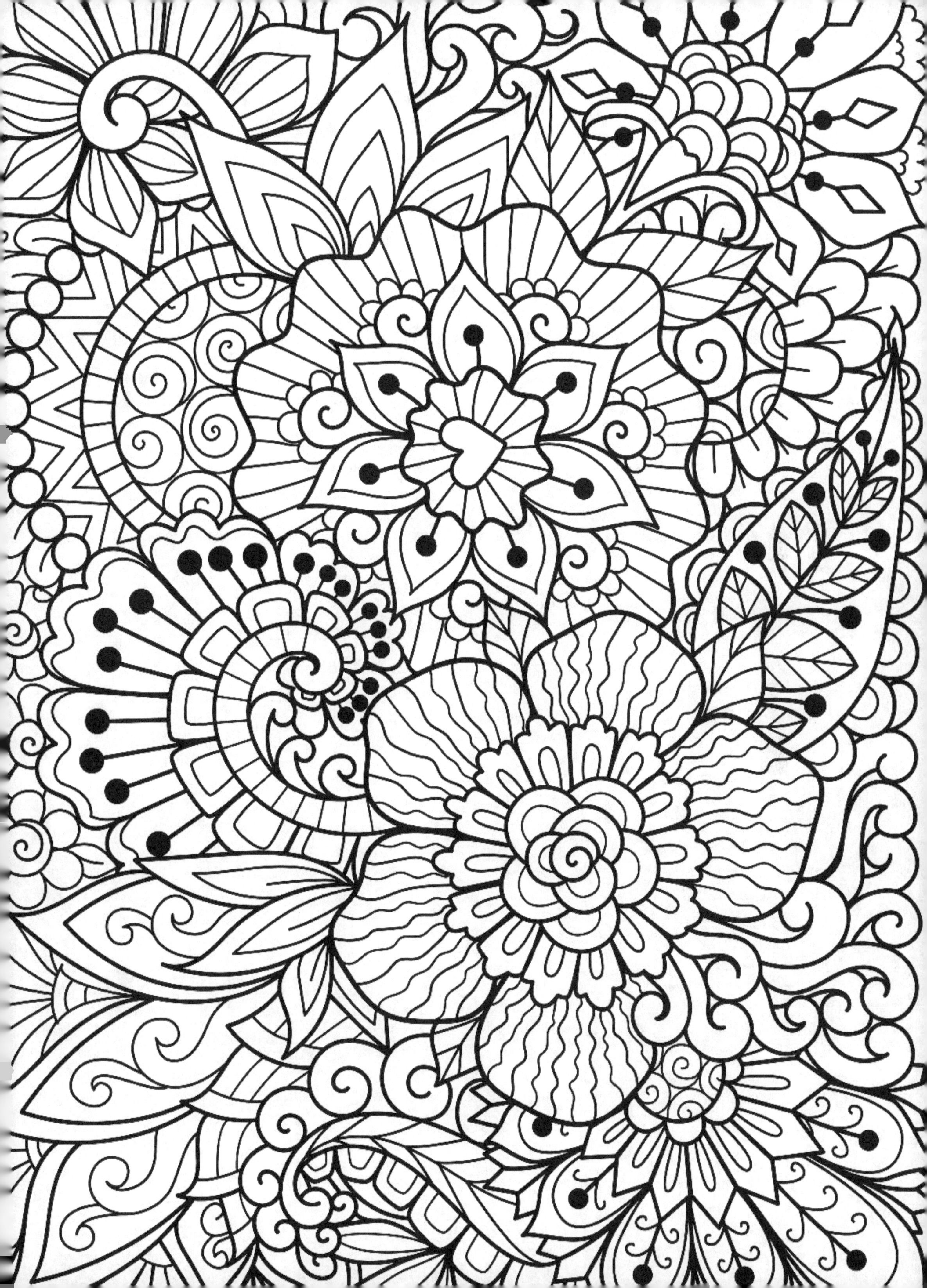

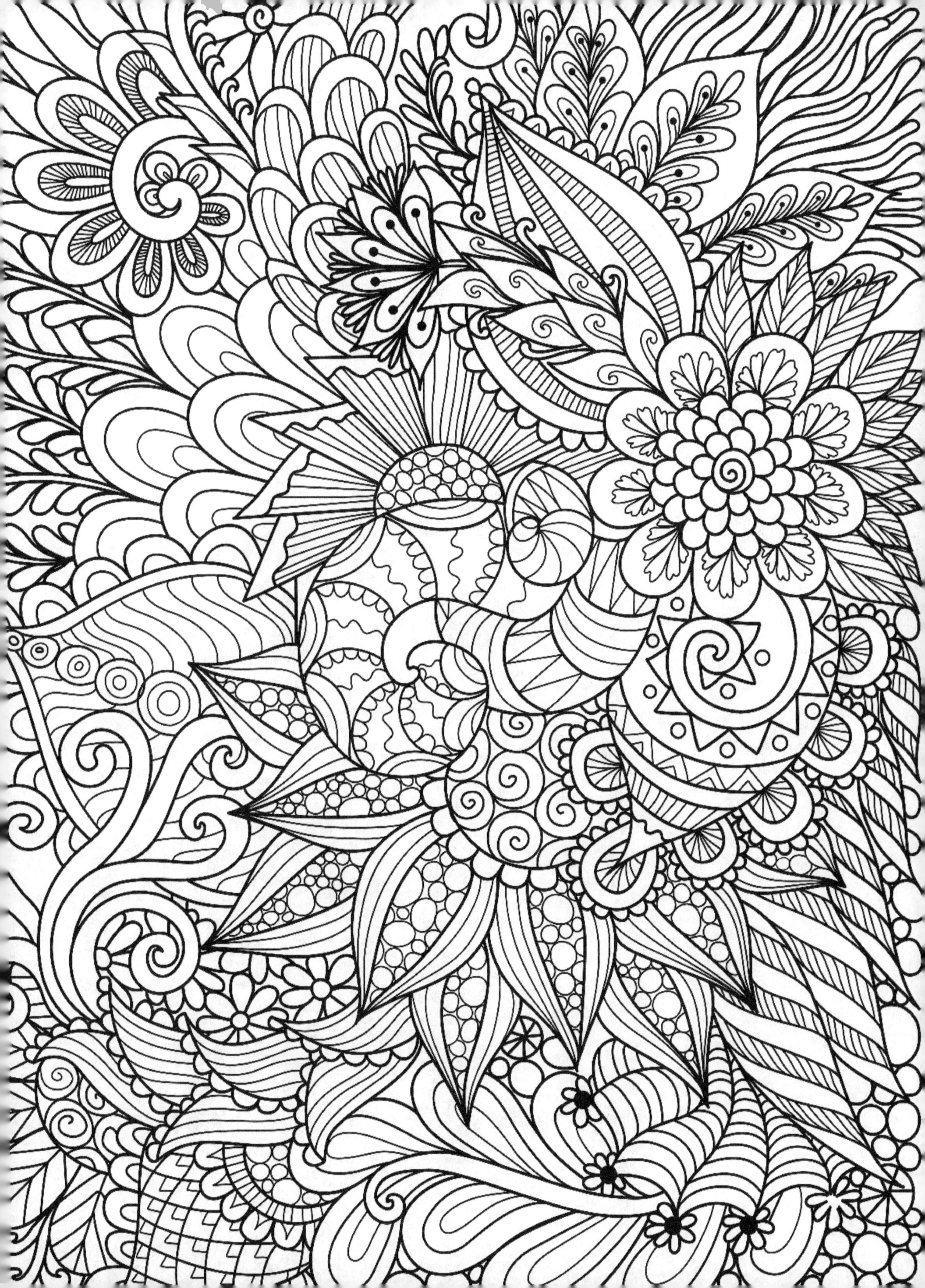

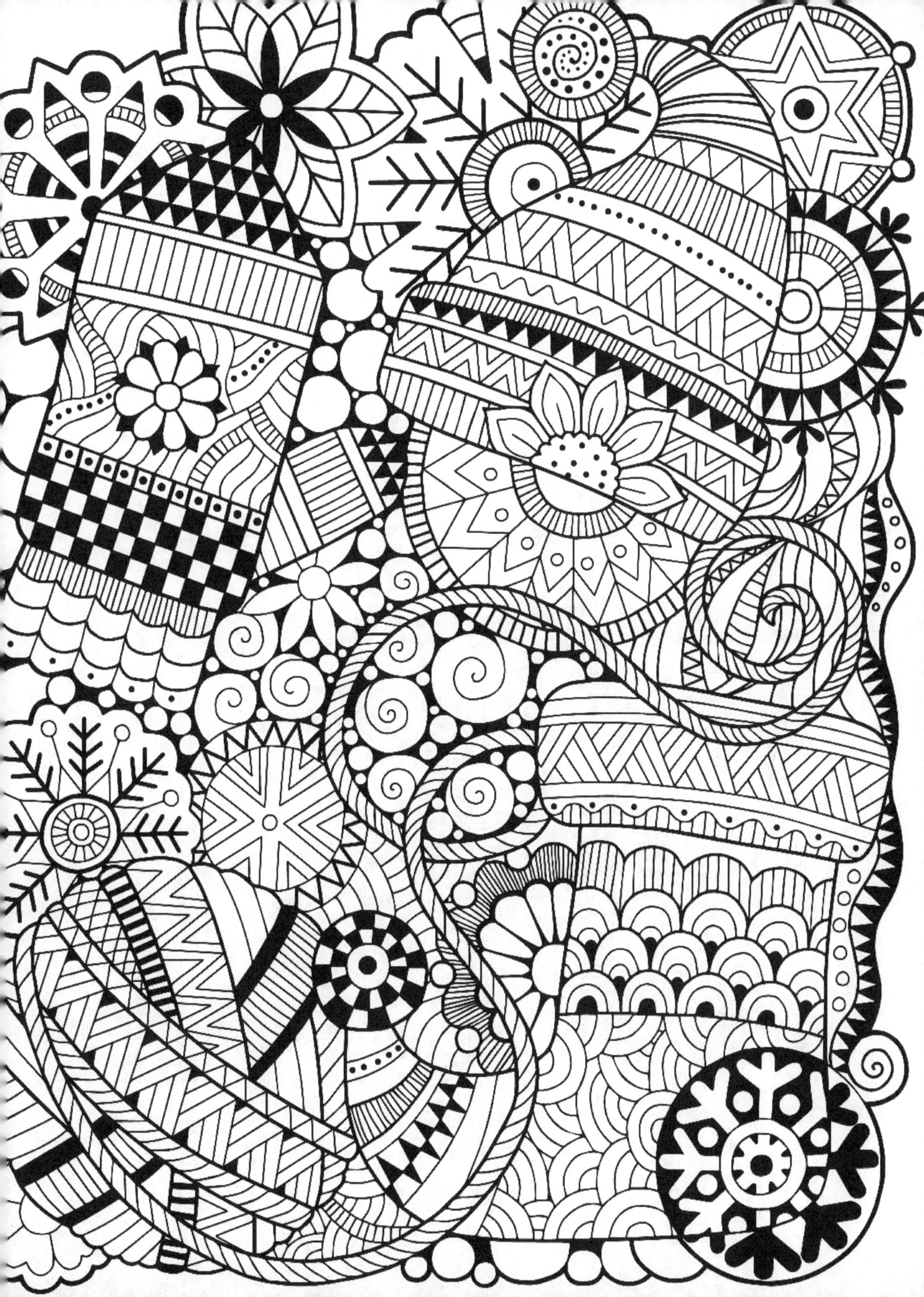

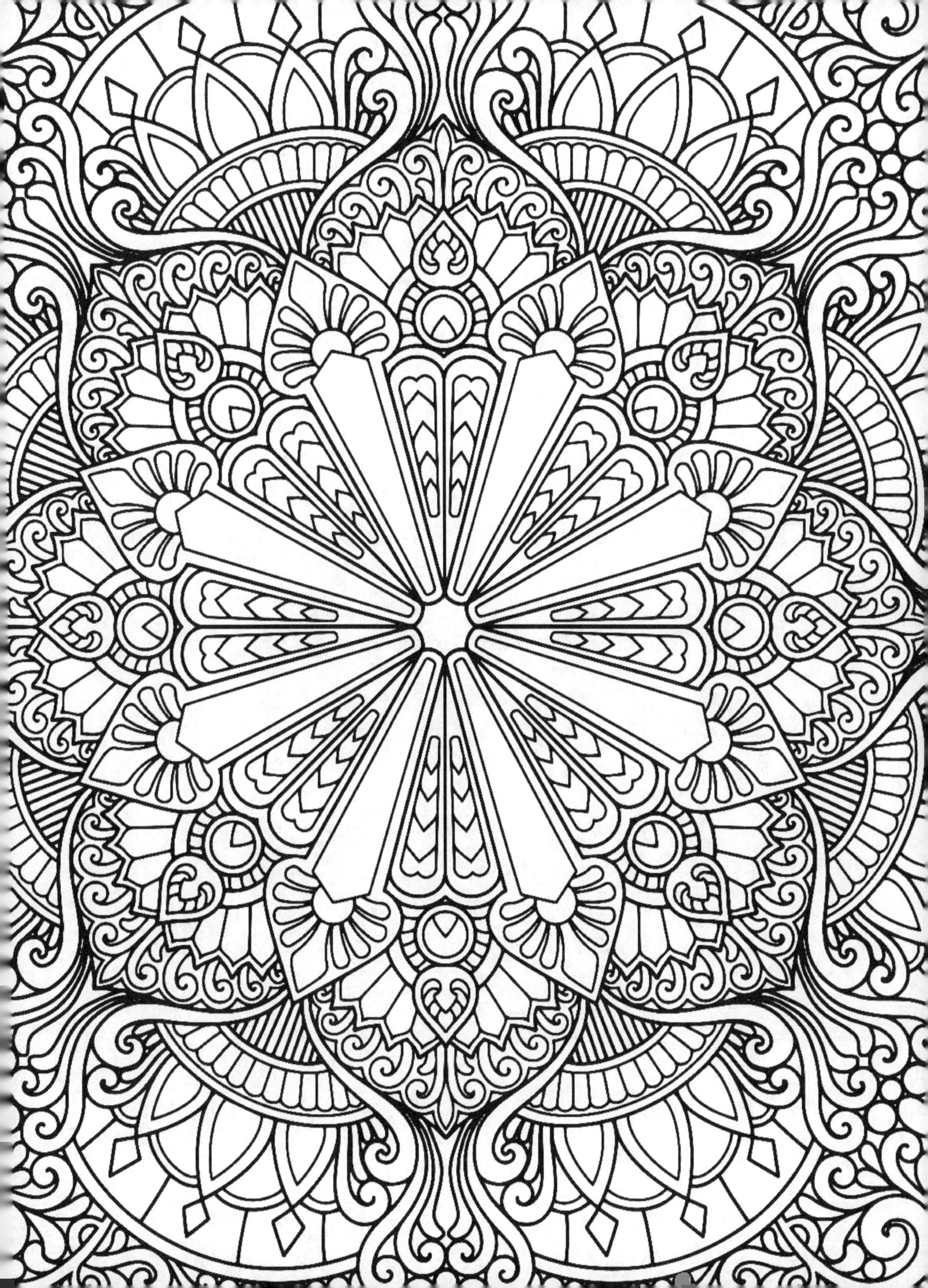

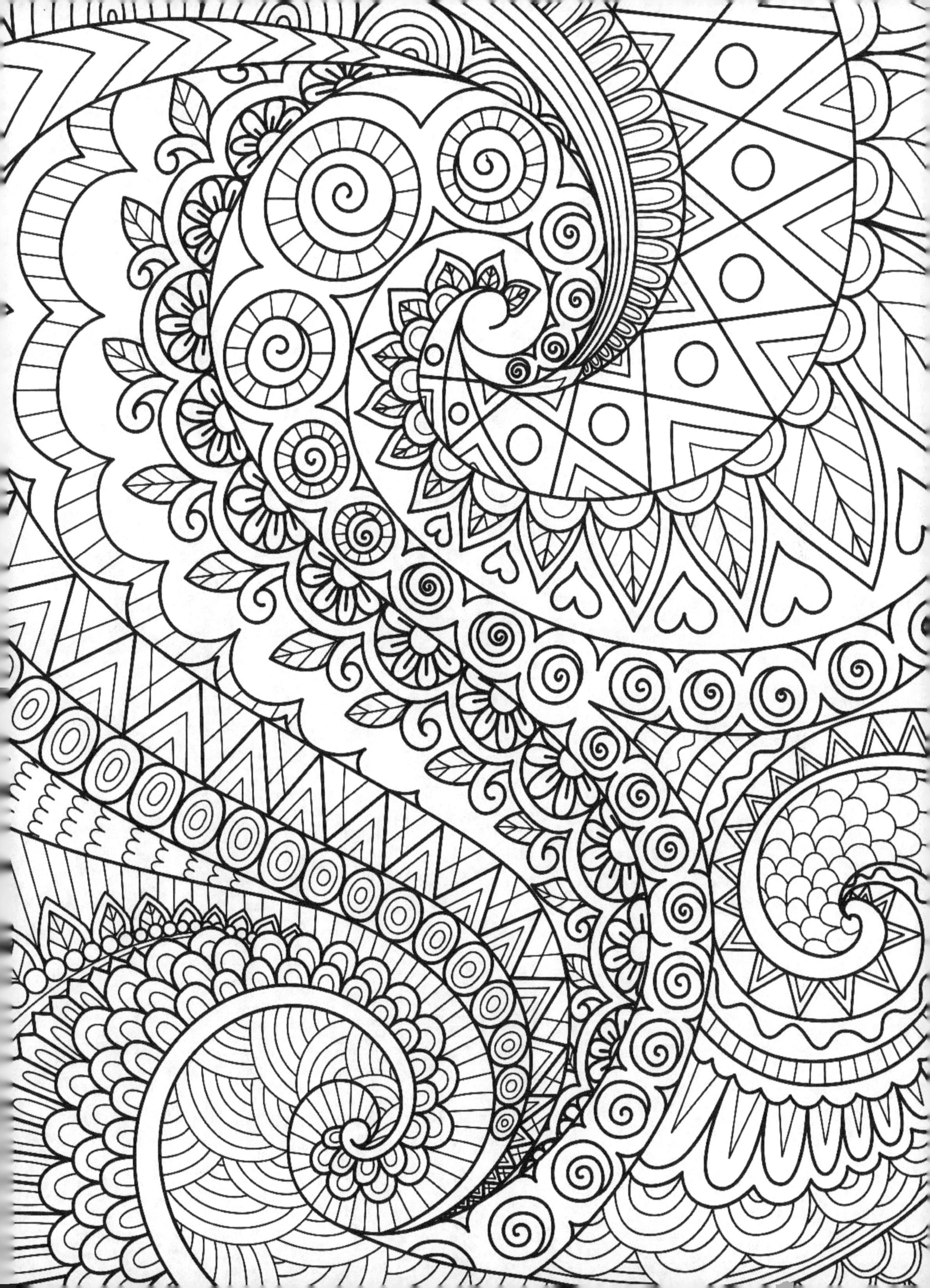

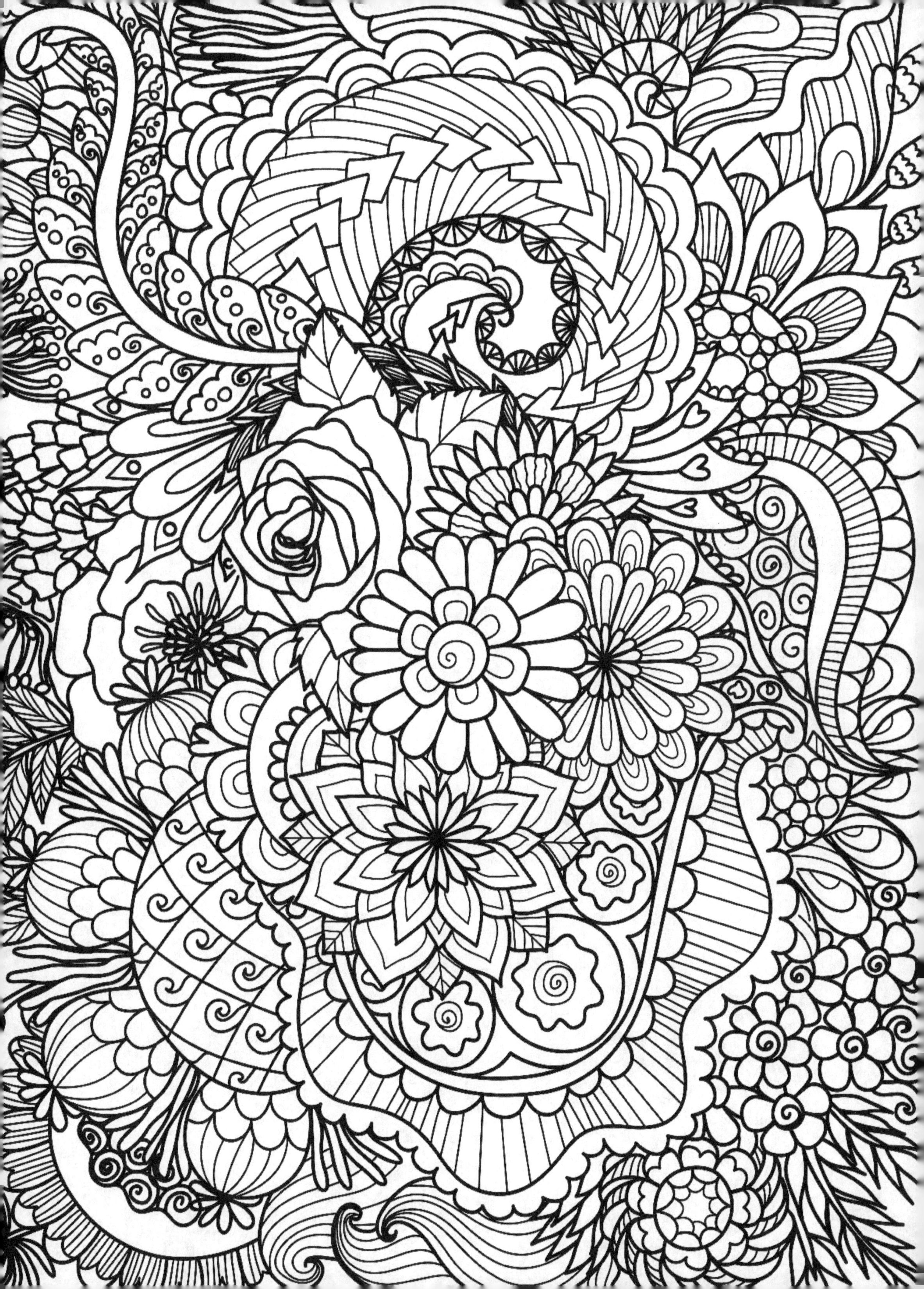

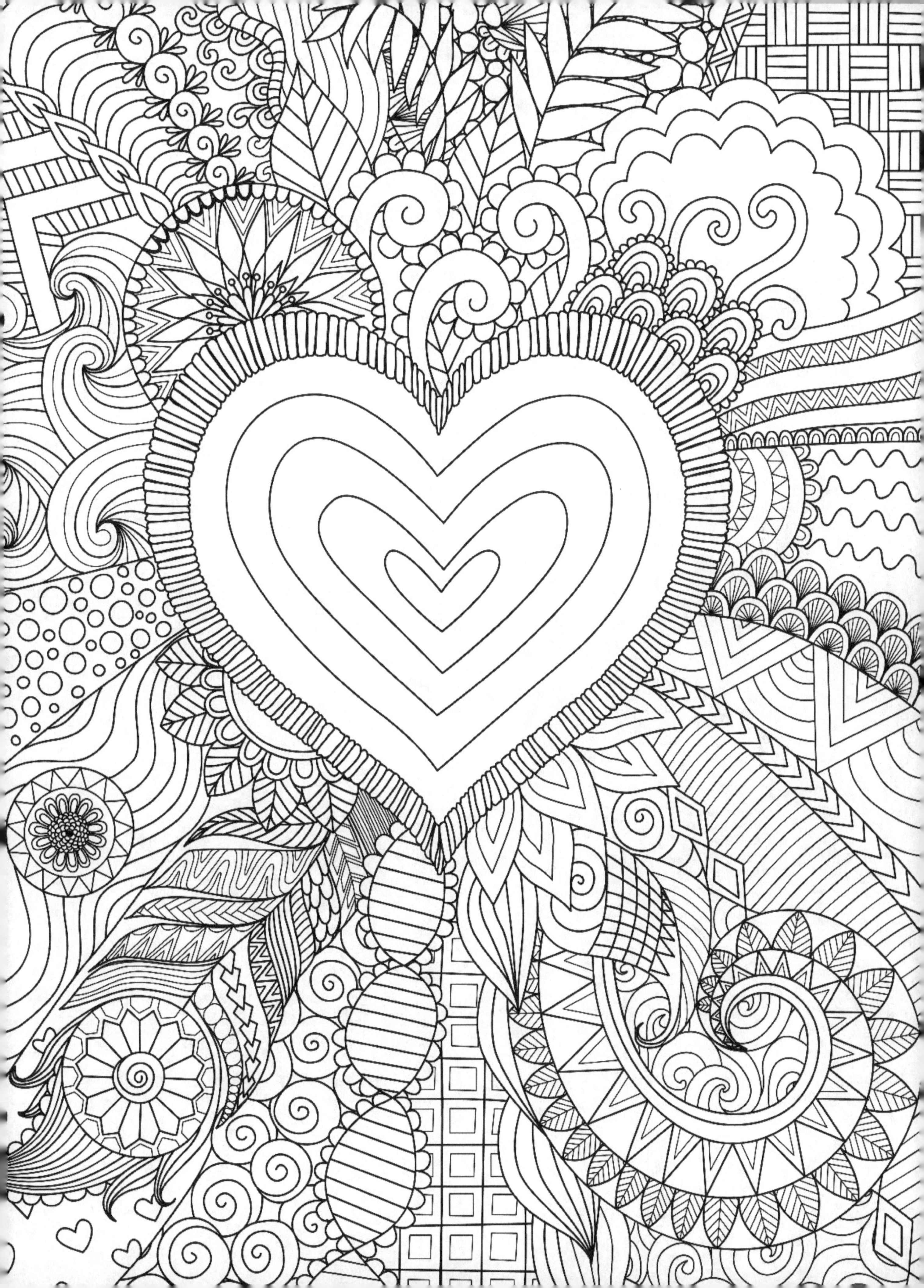

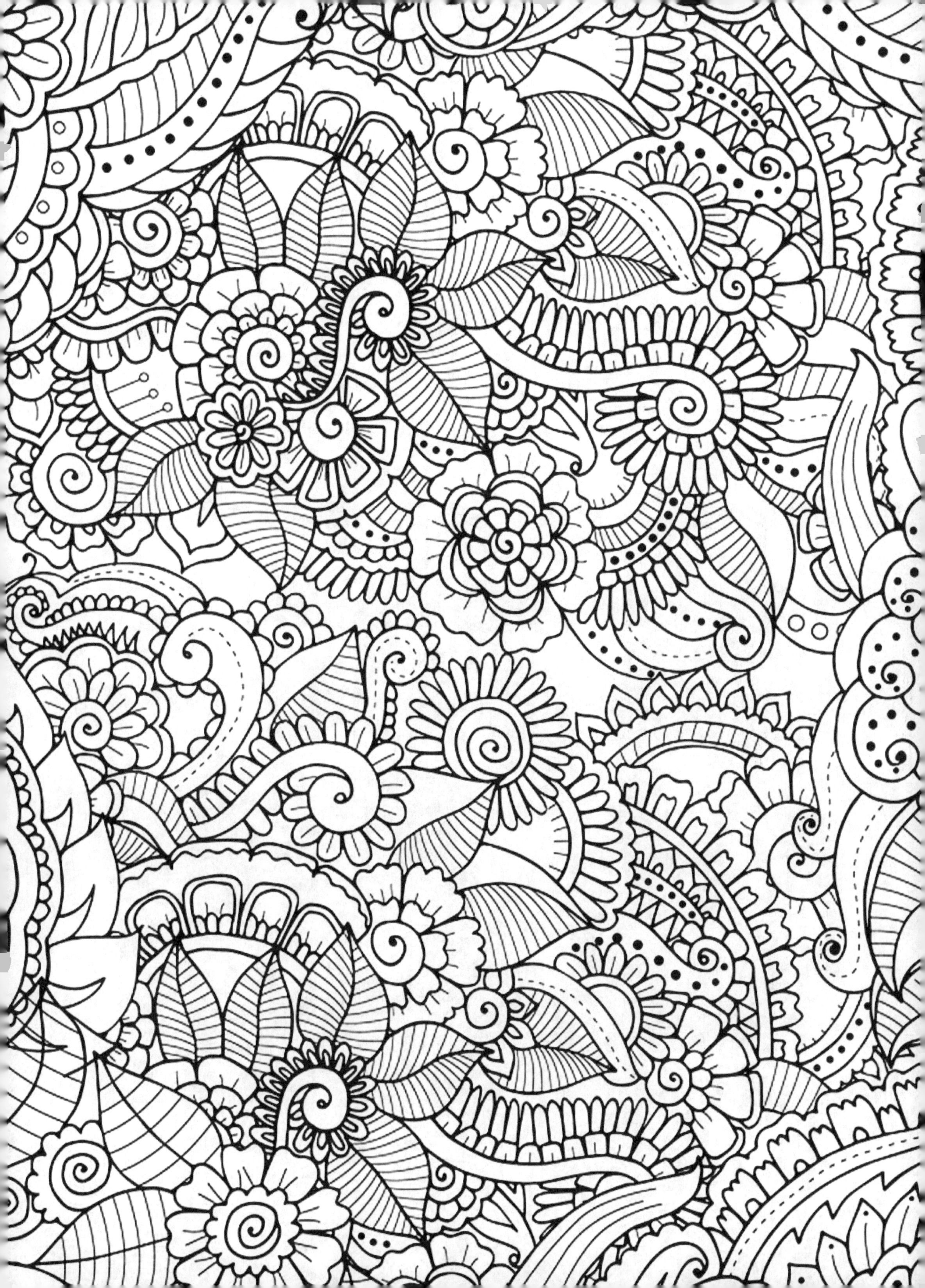

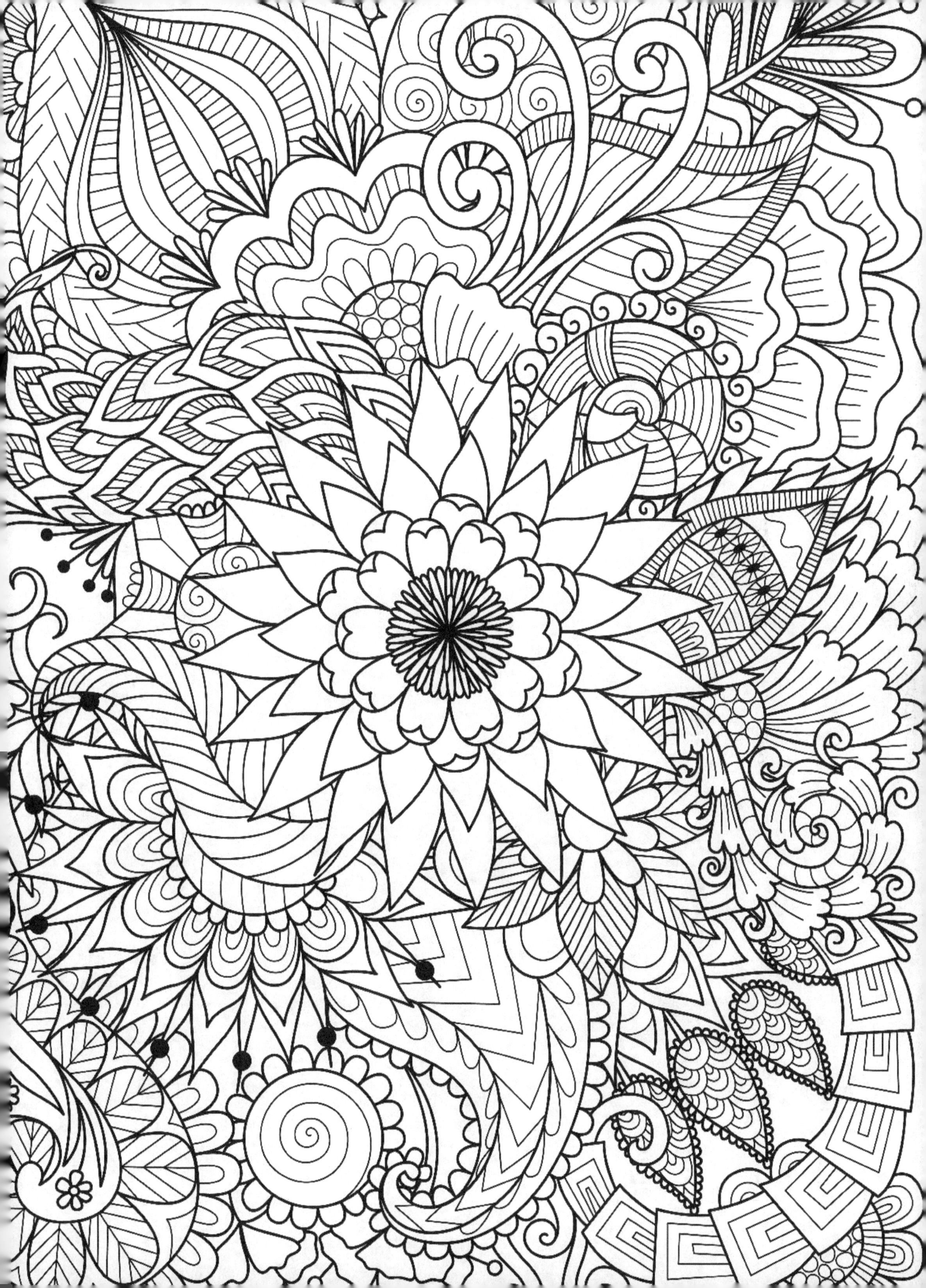

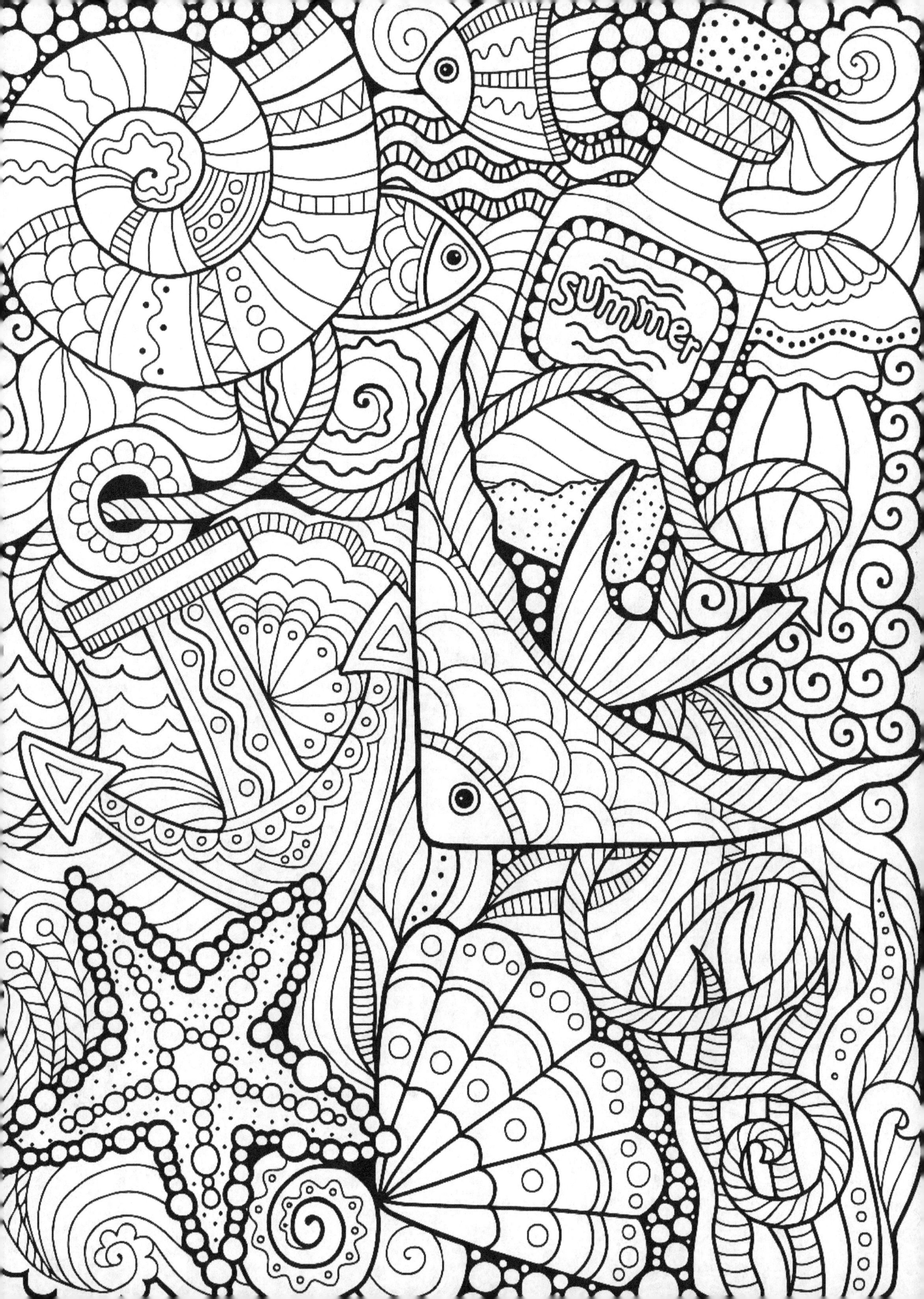
summer

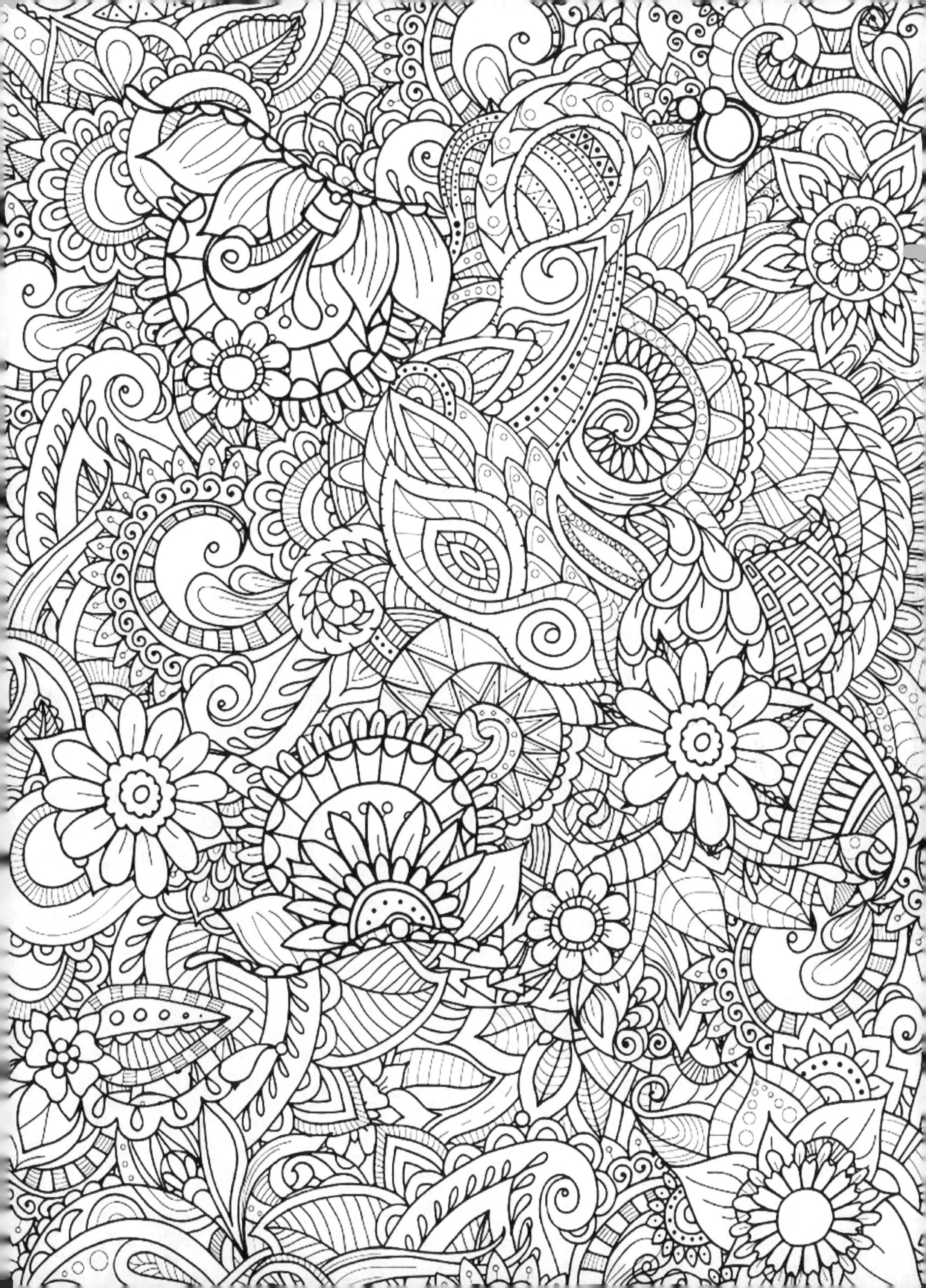

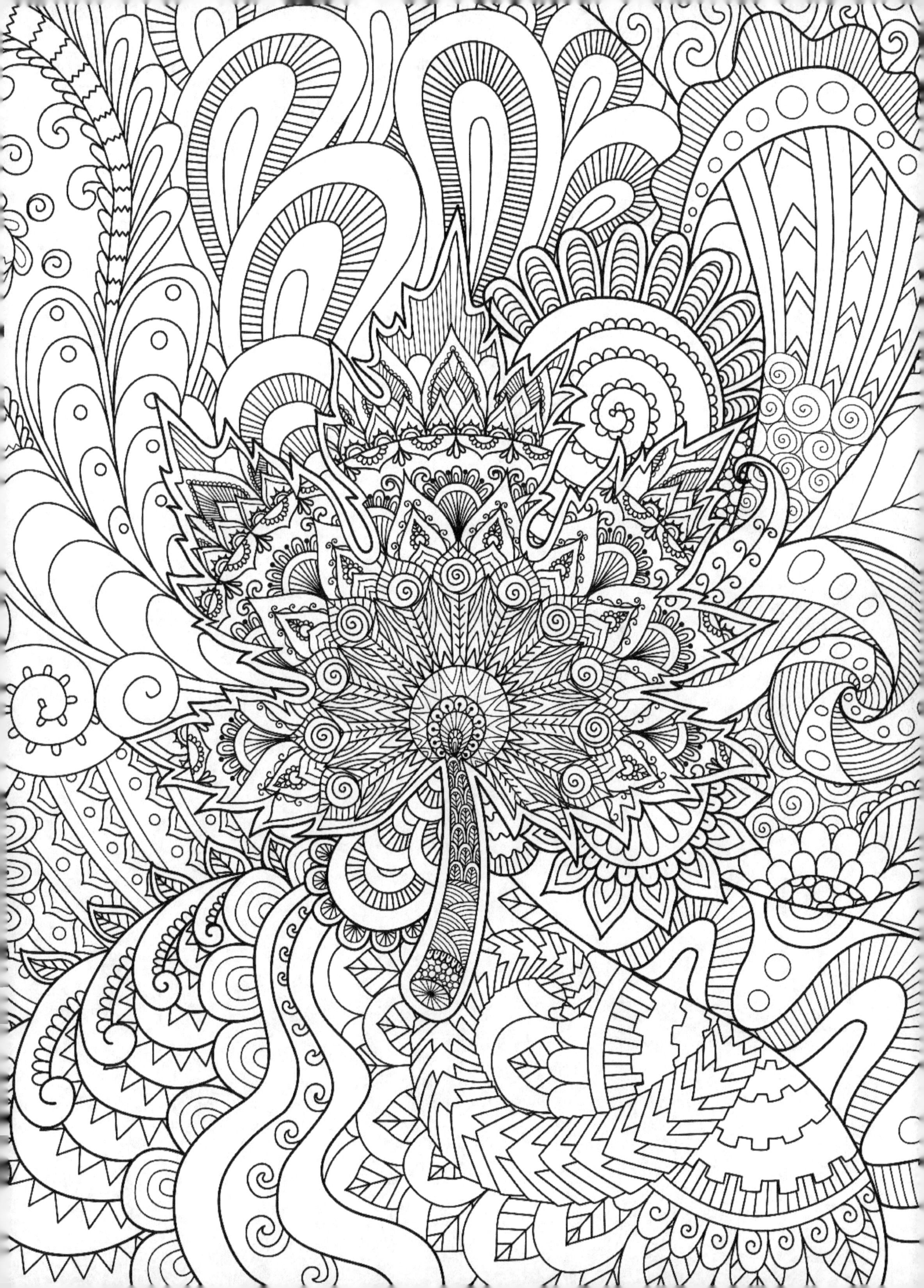

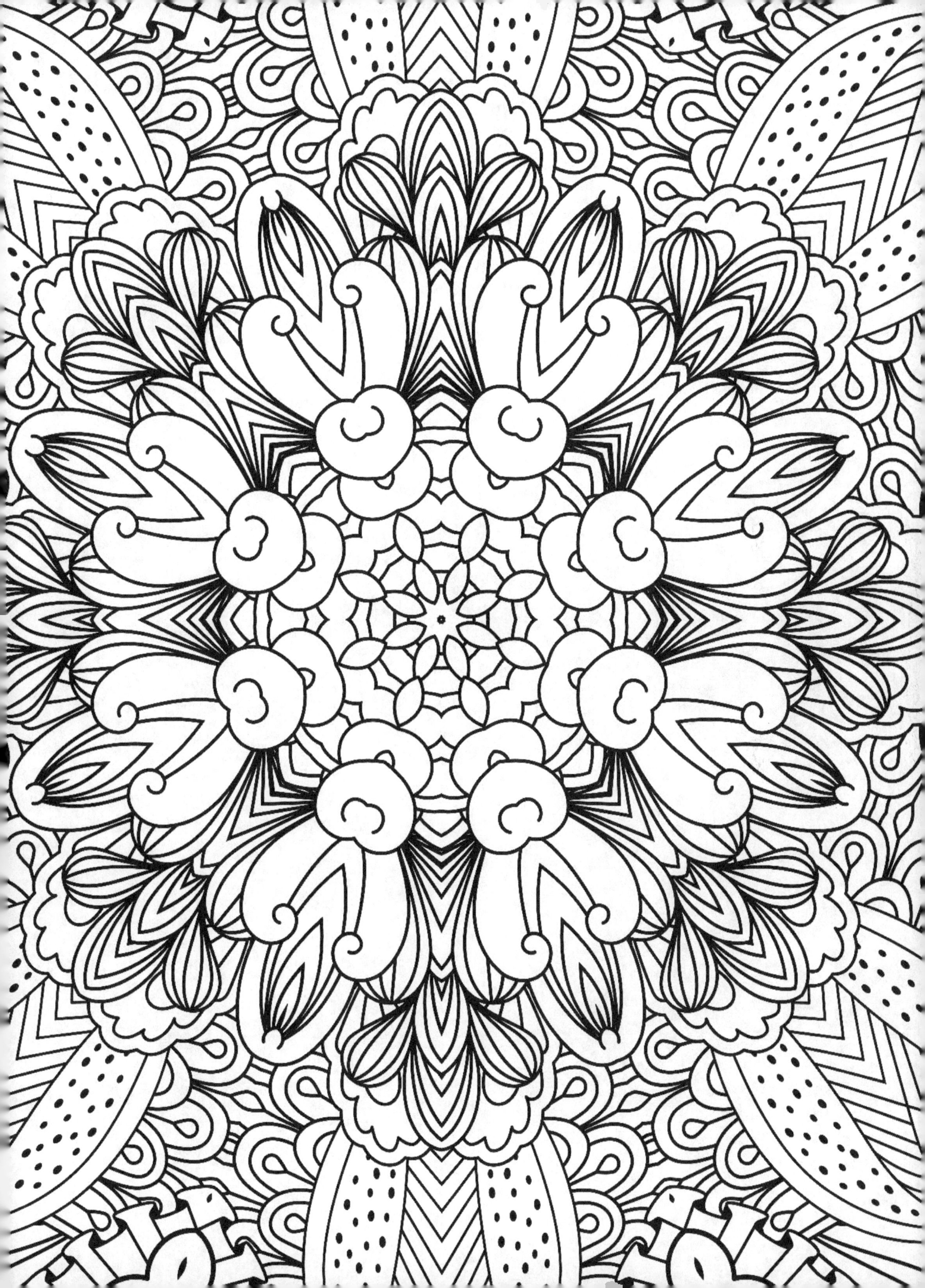

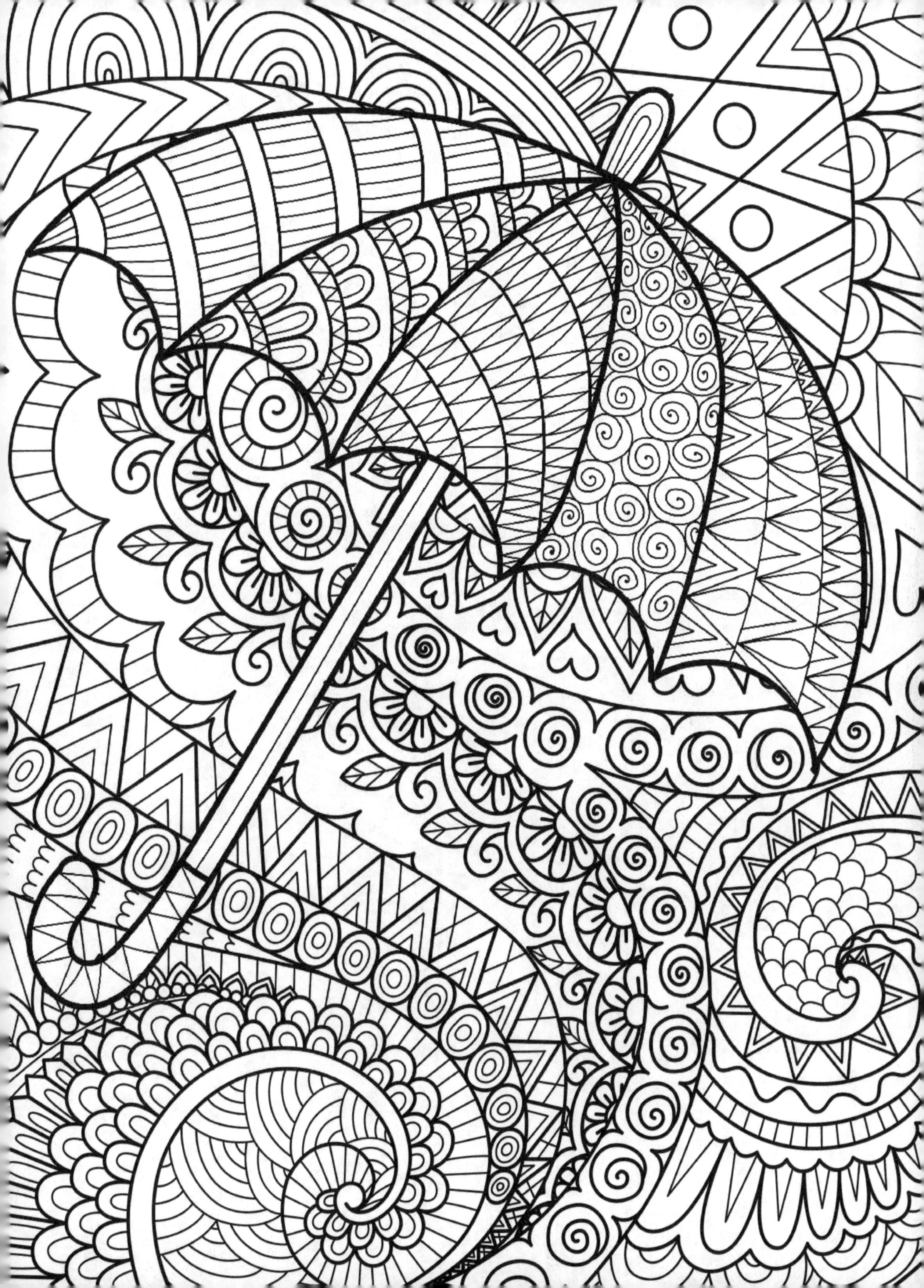

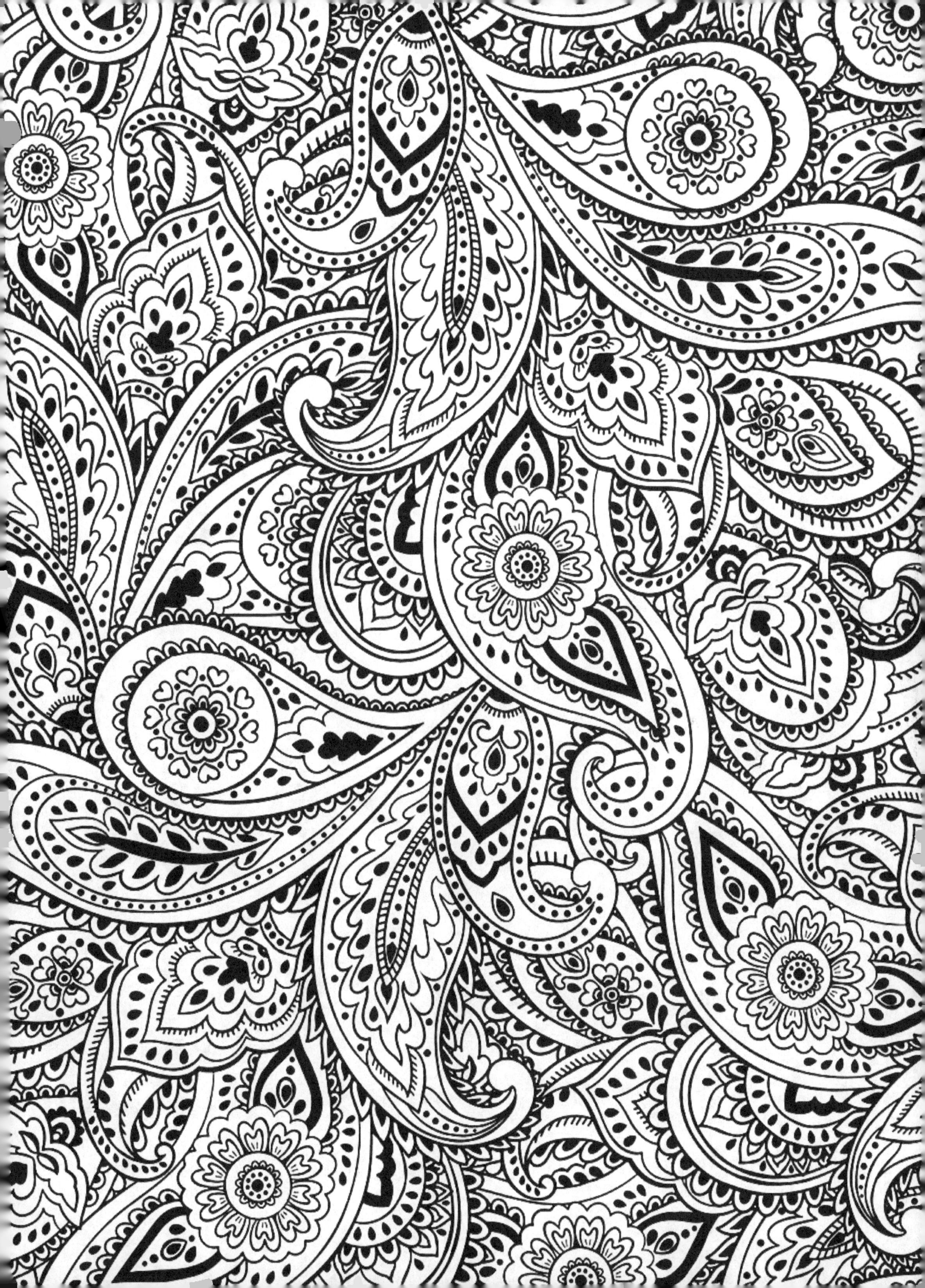

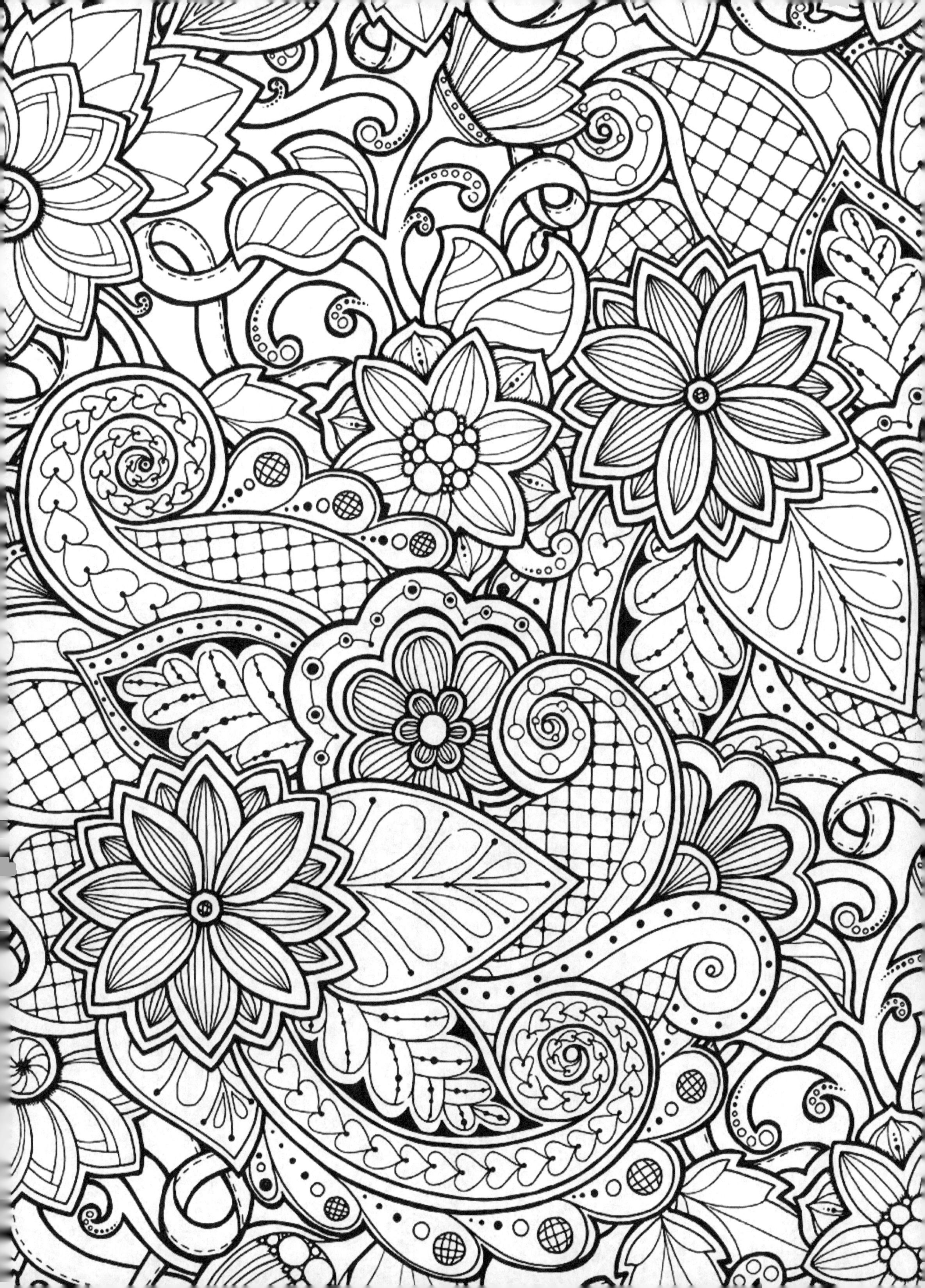

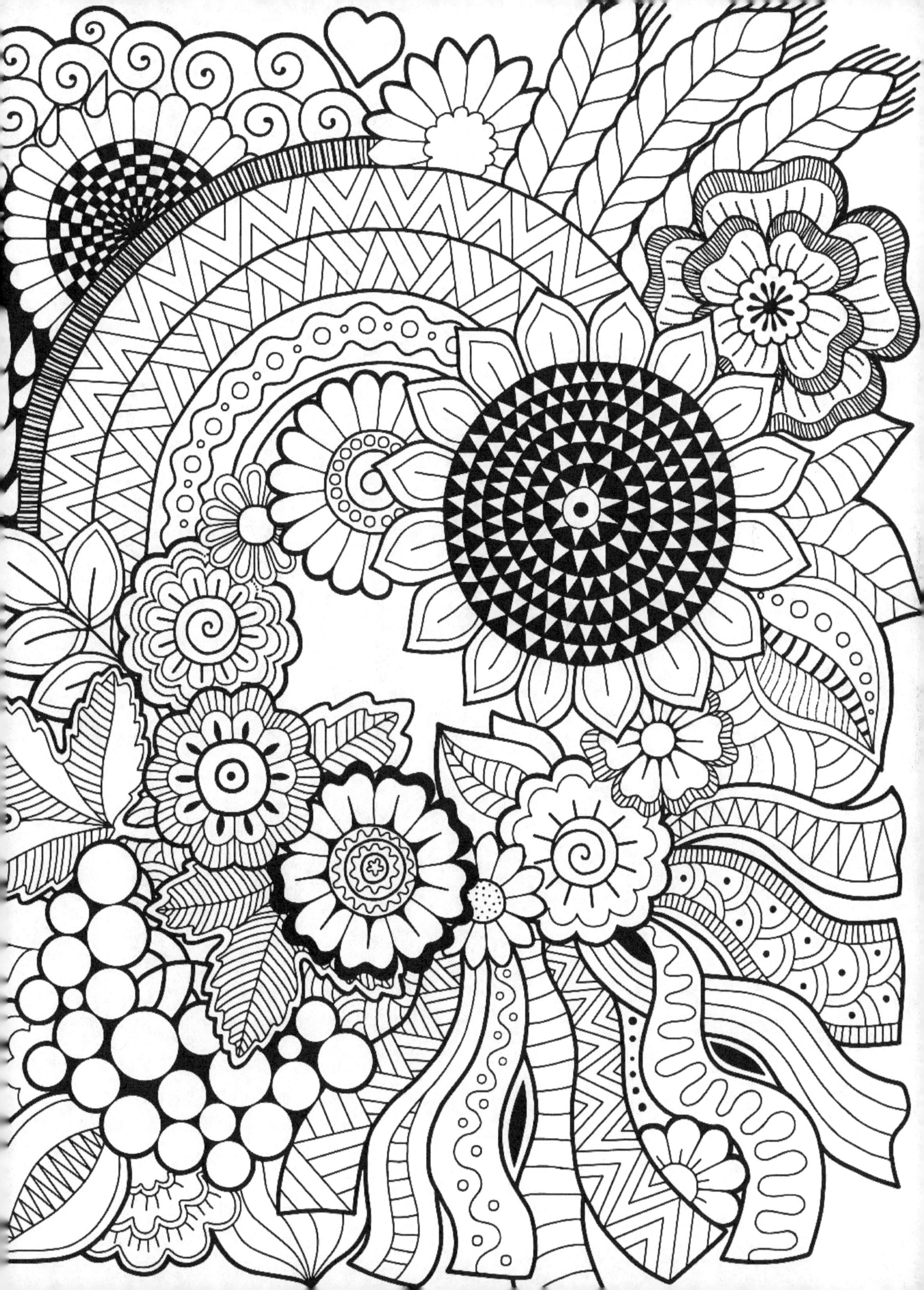

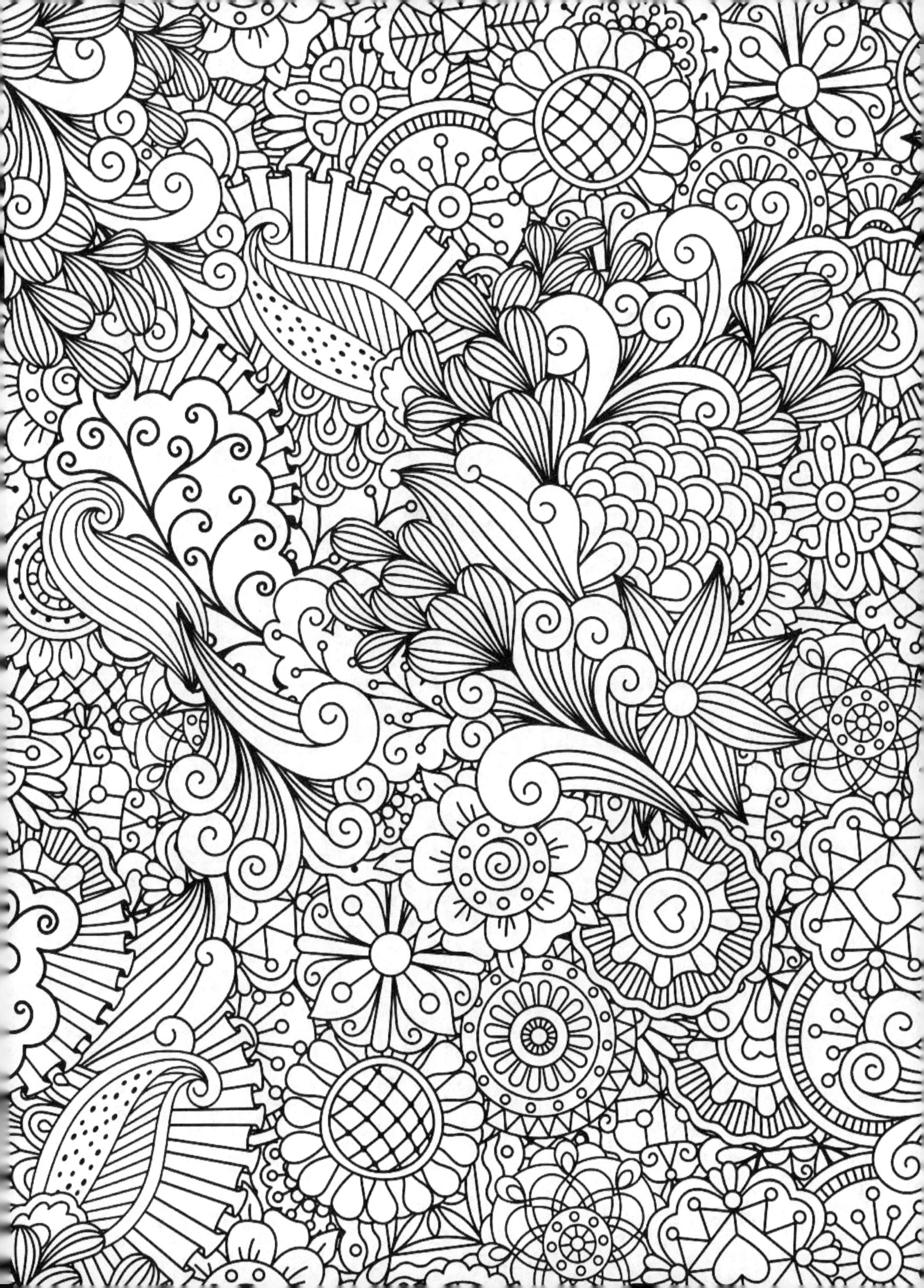

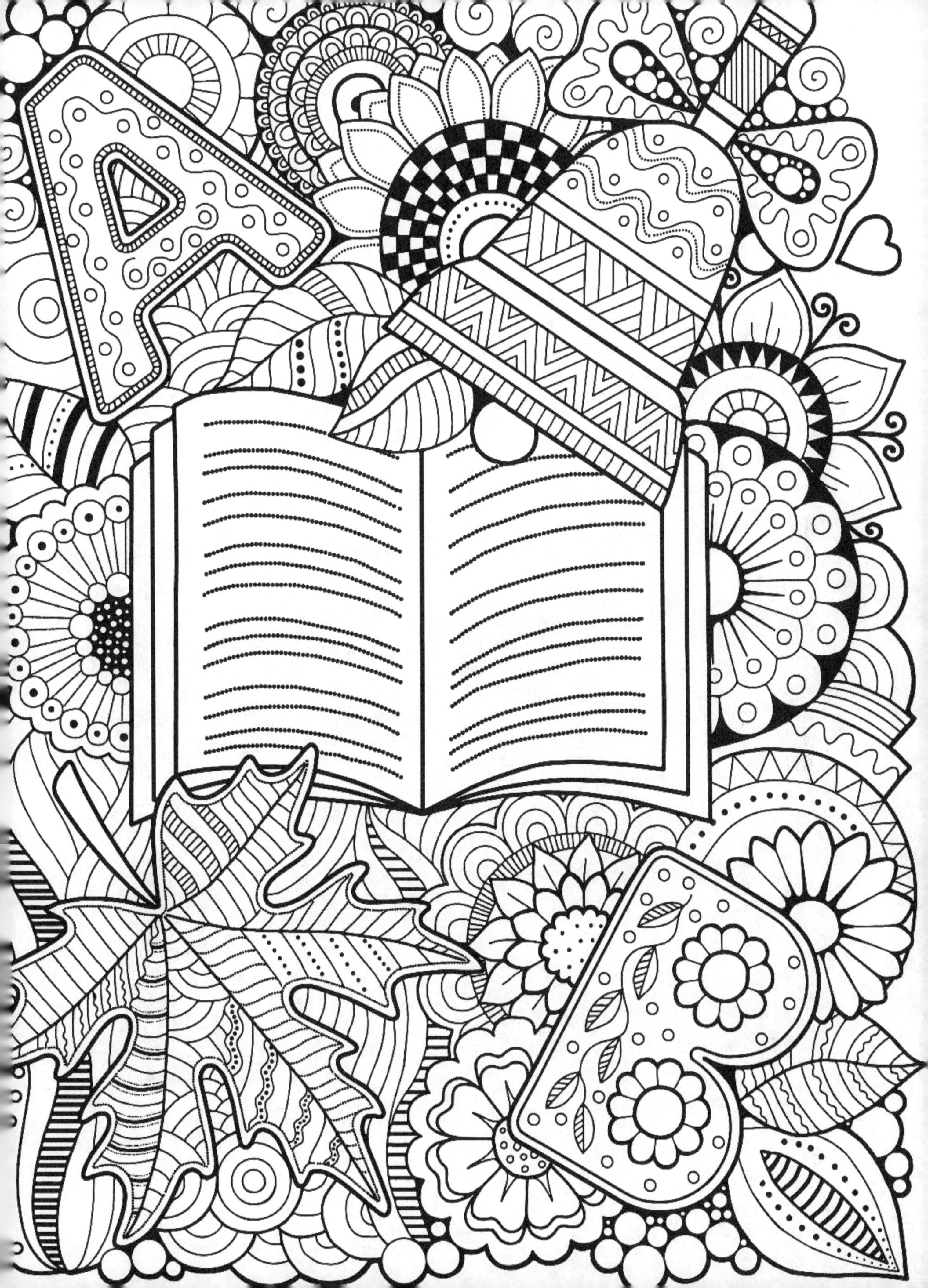

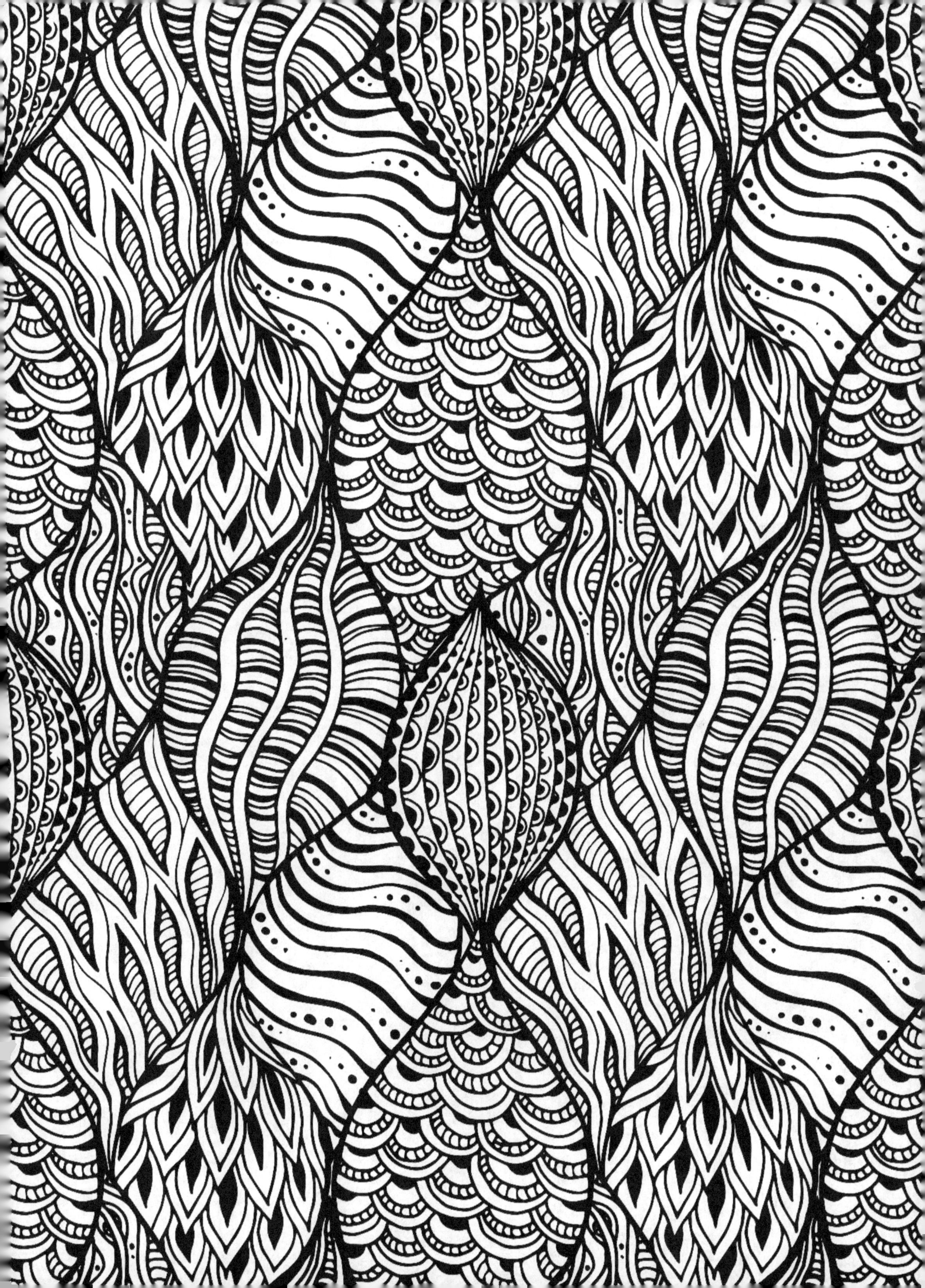

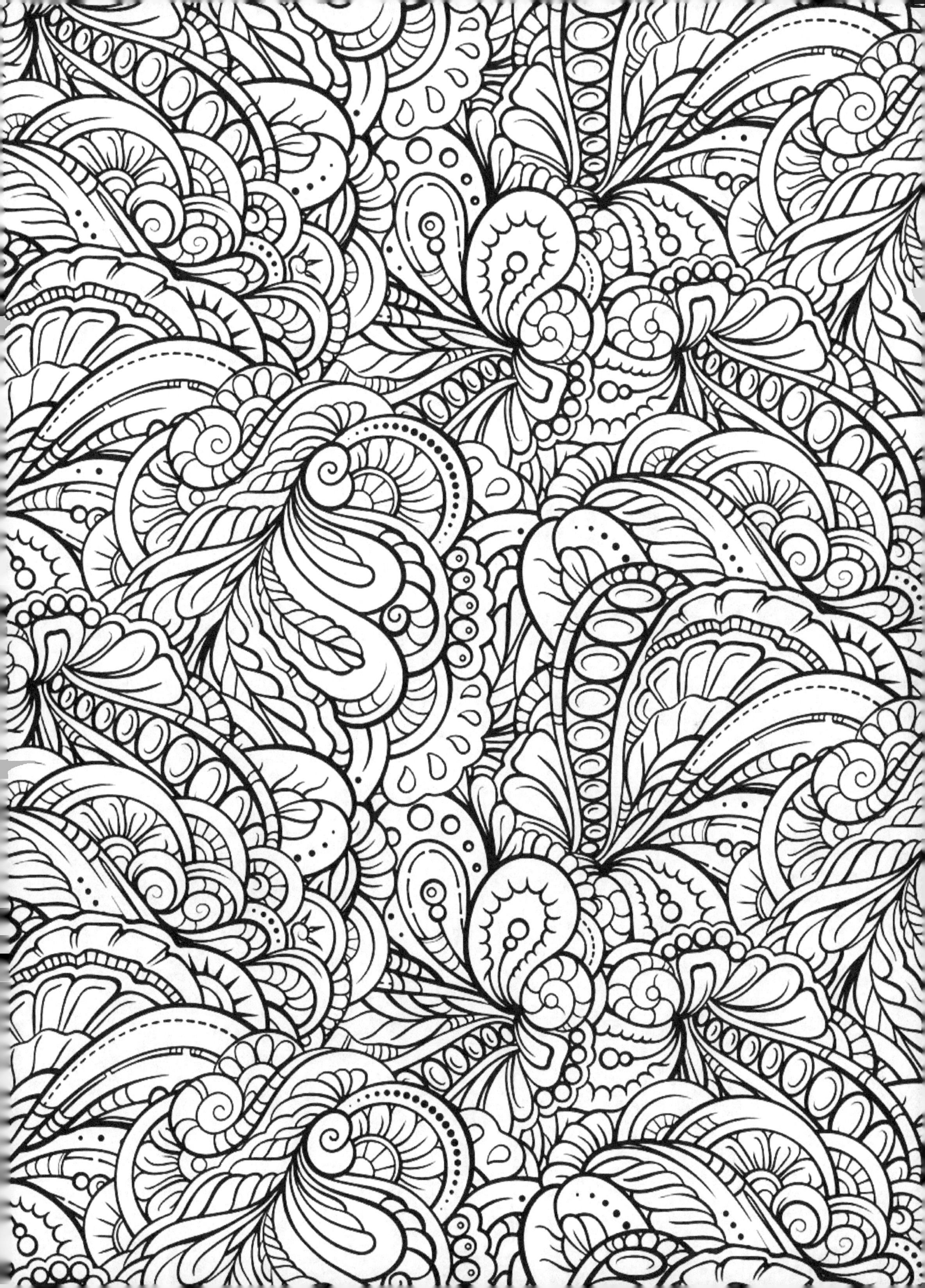

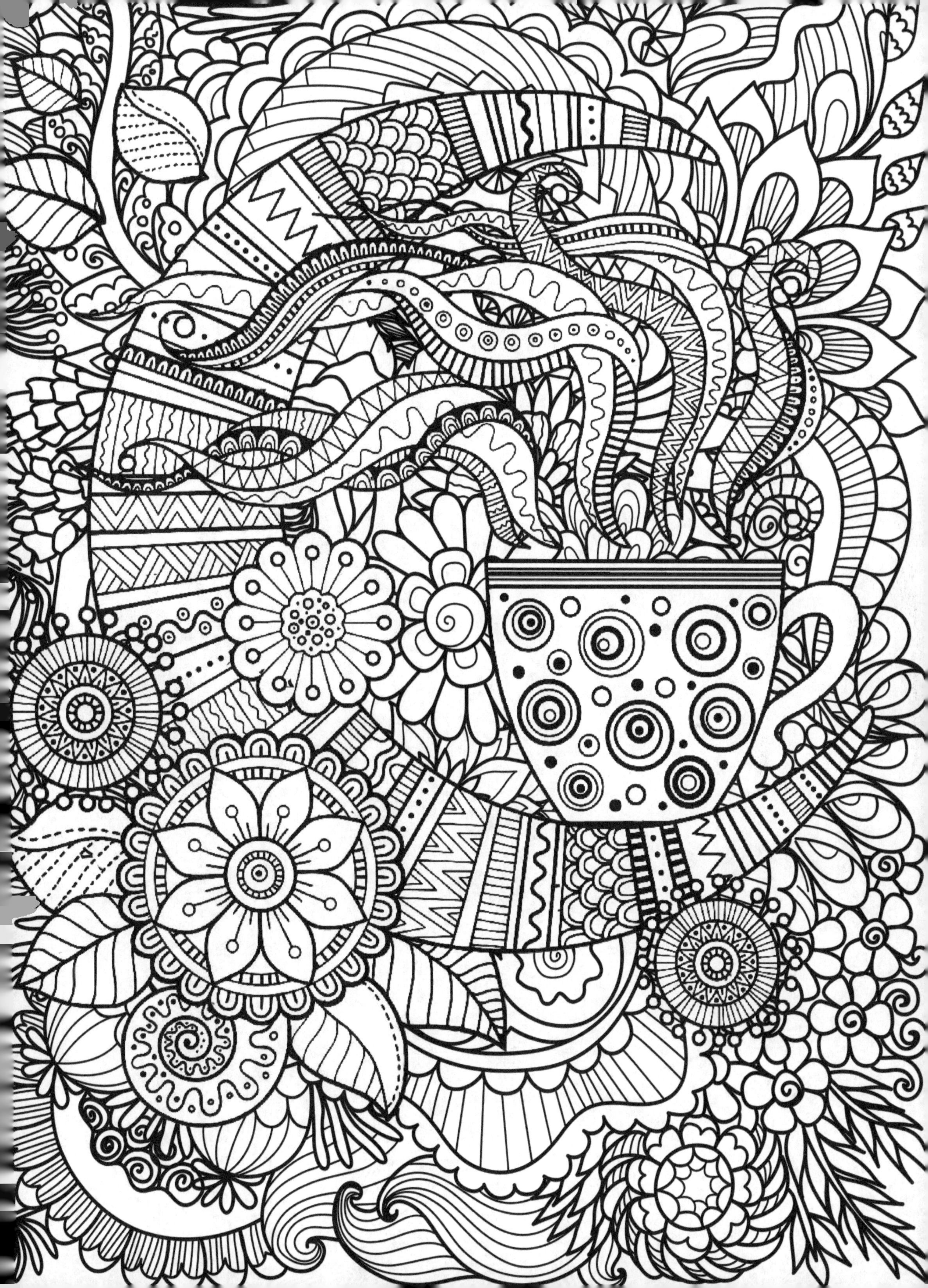

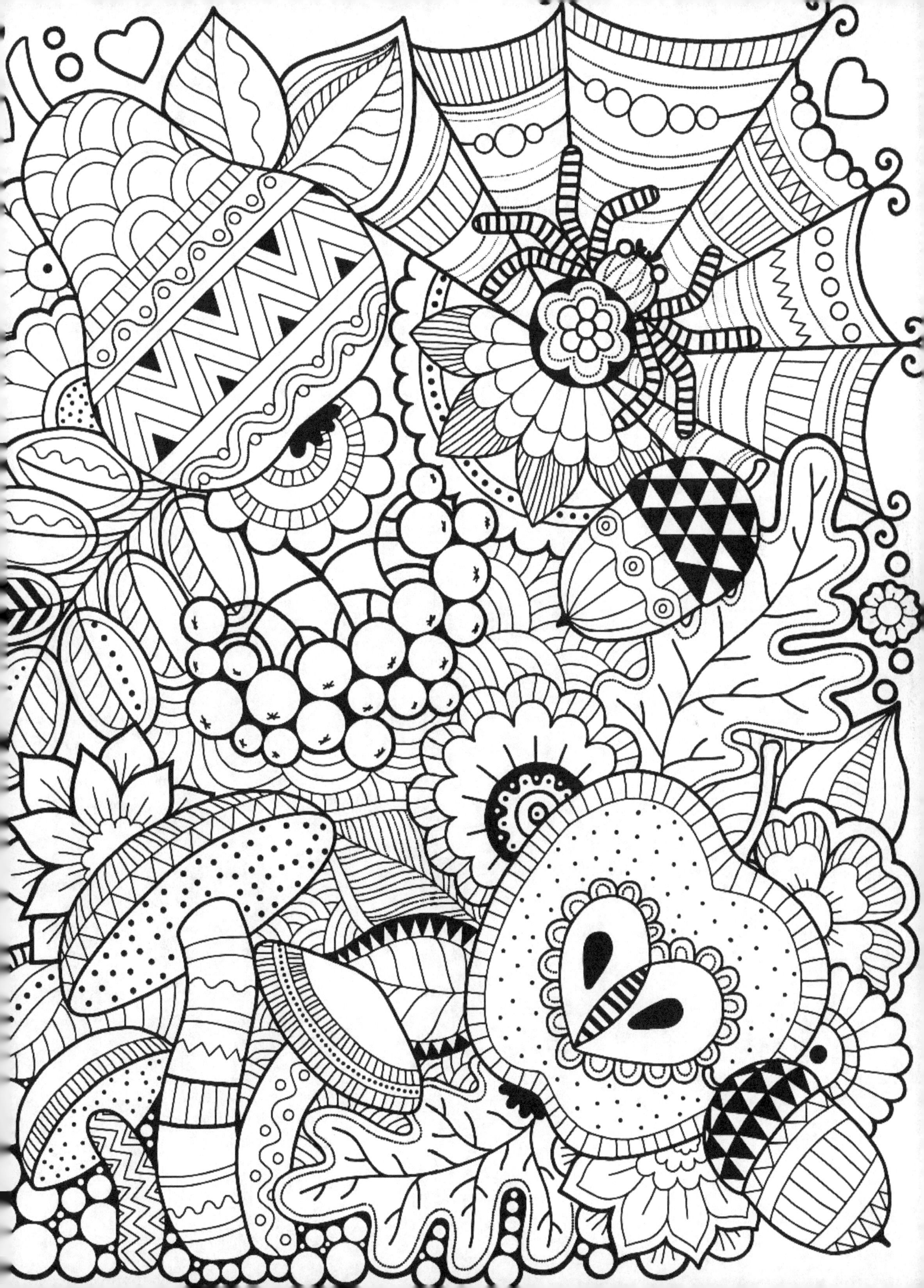

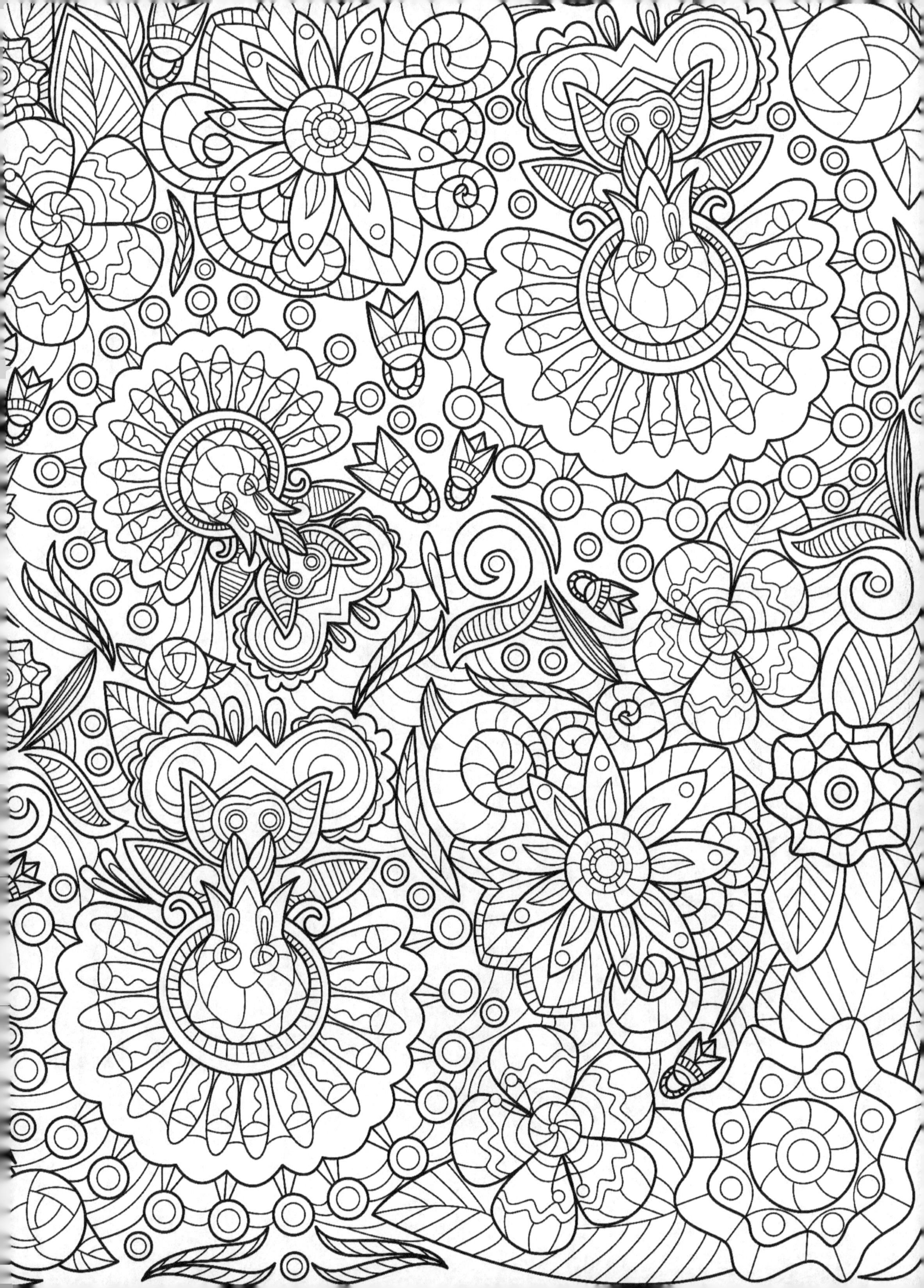

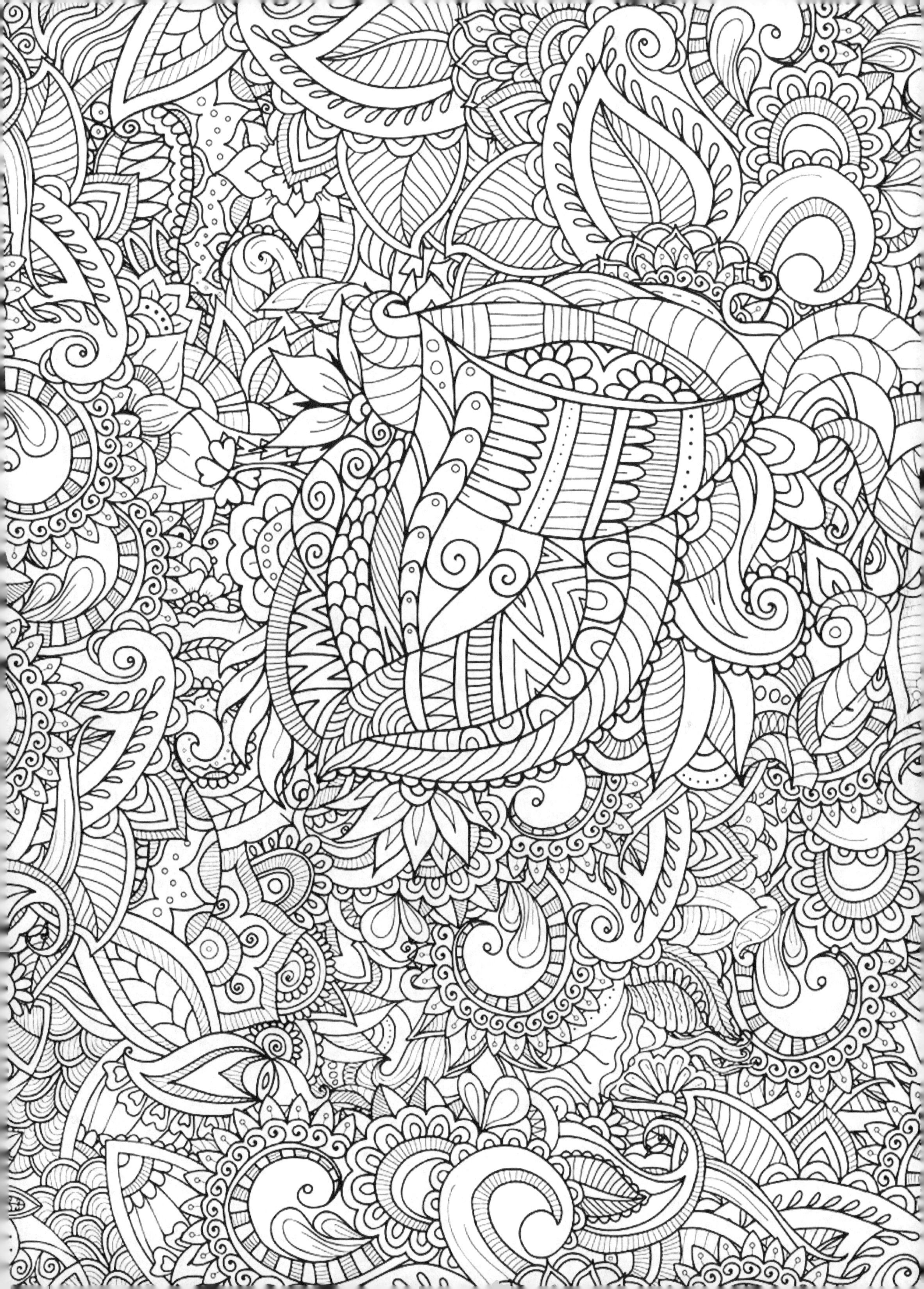

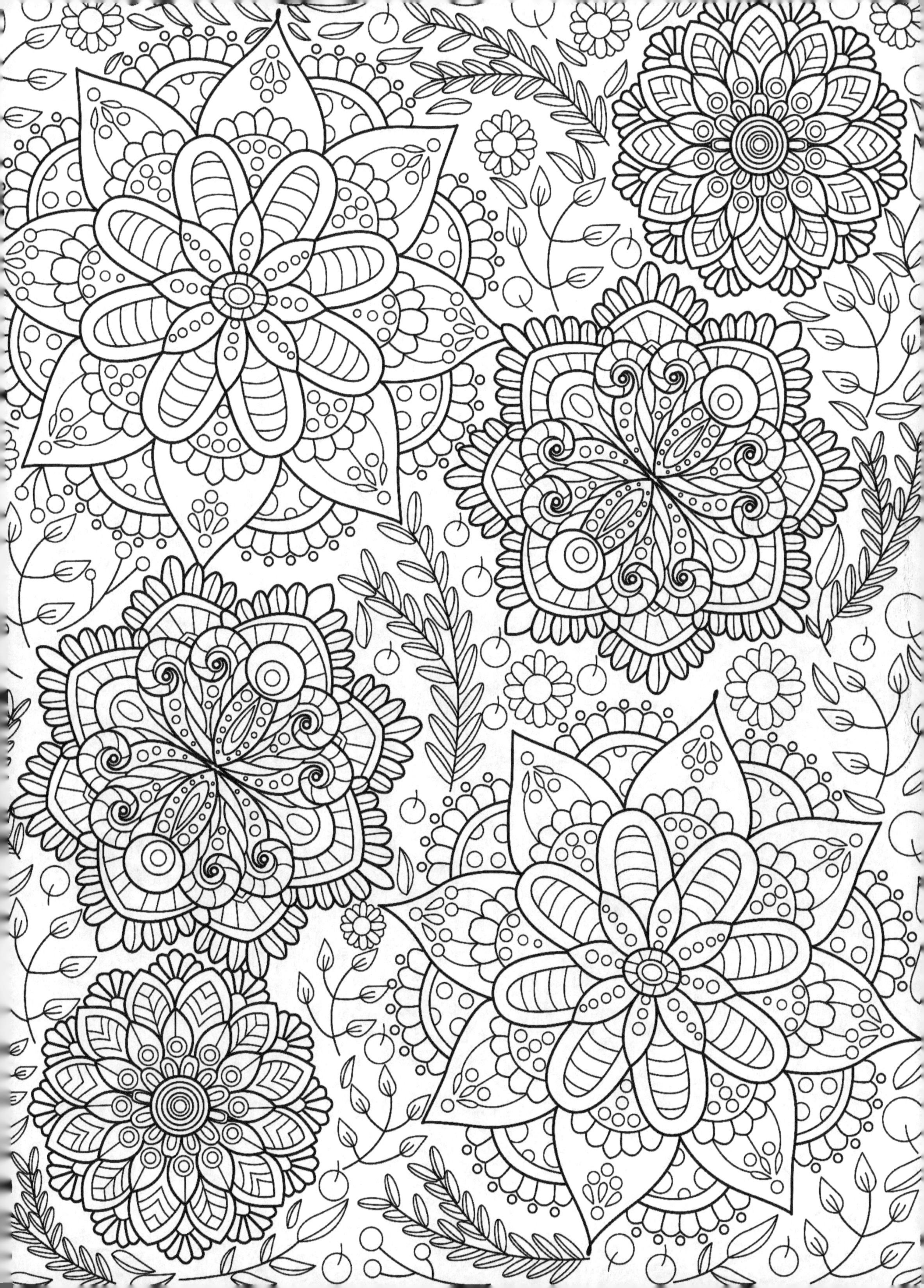

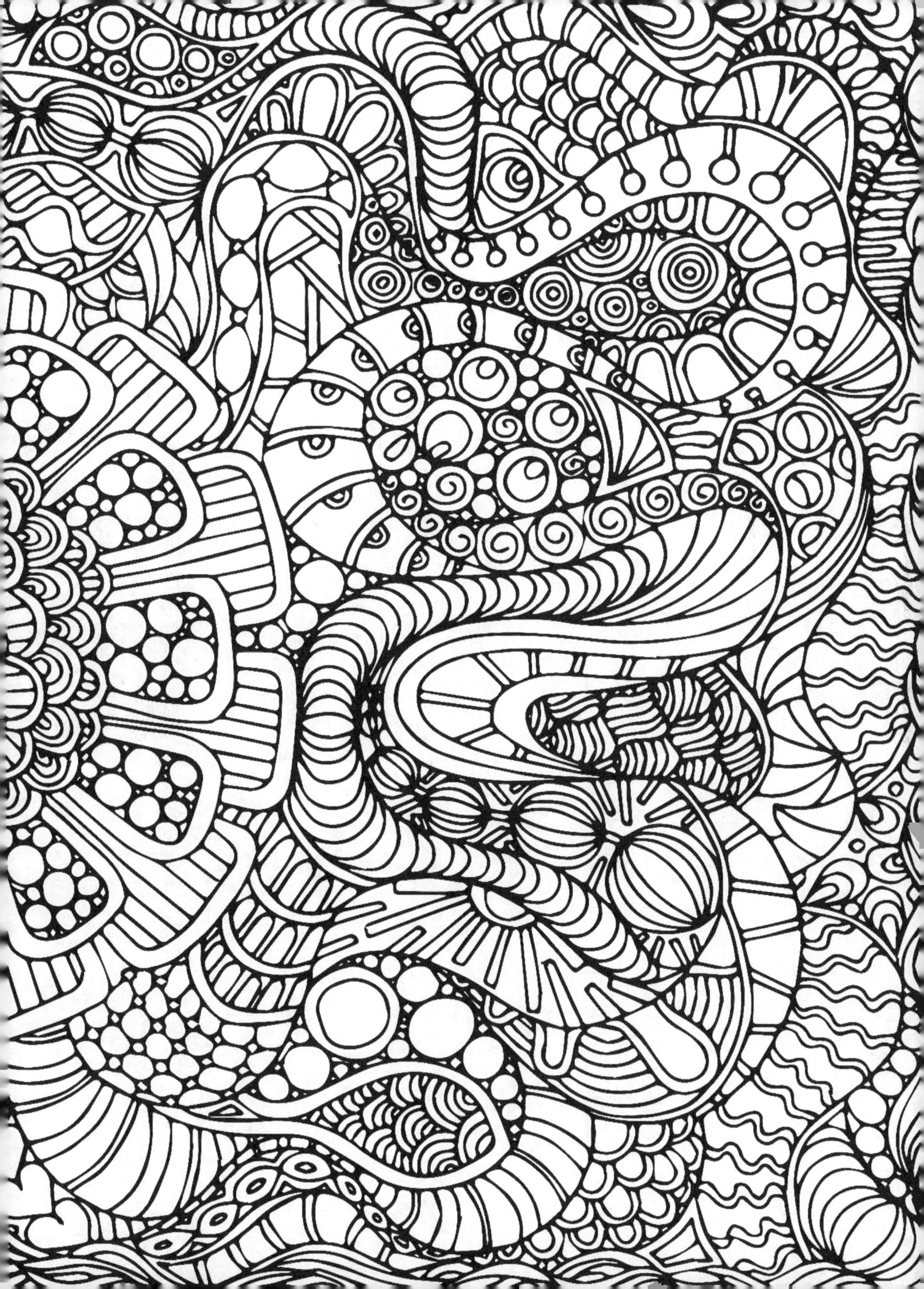

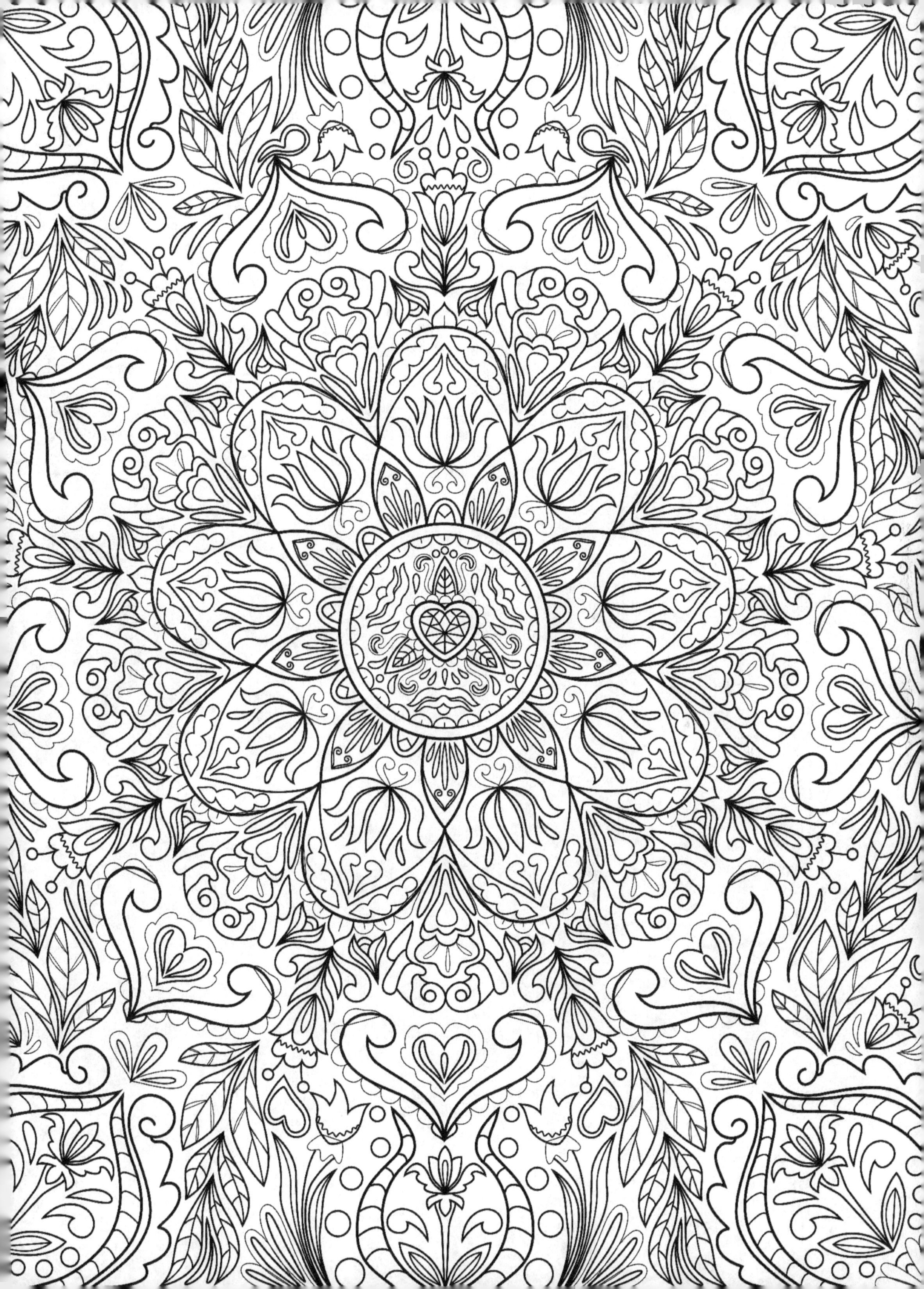

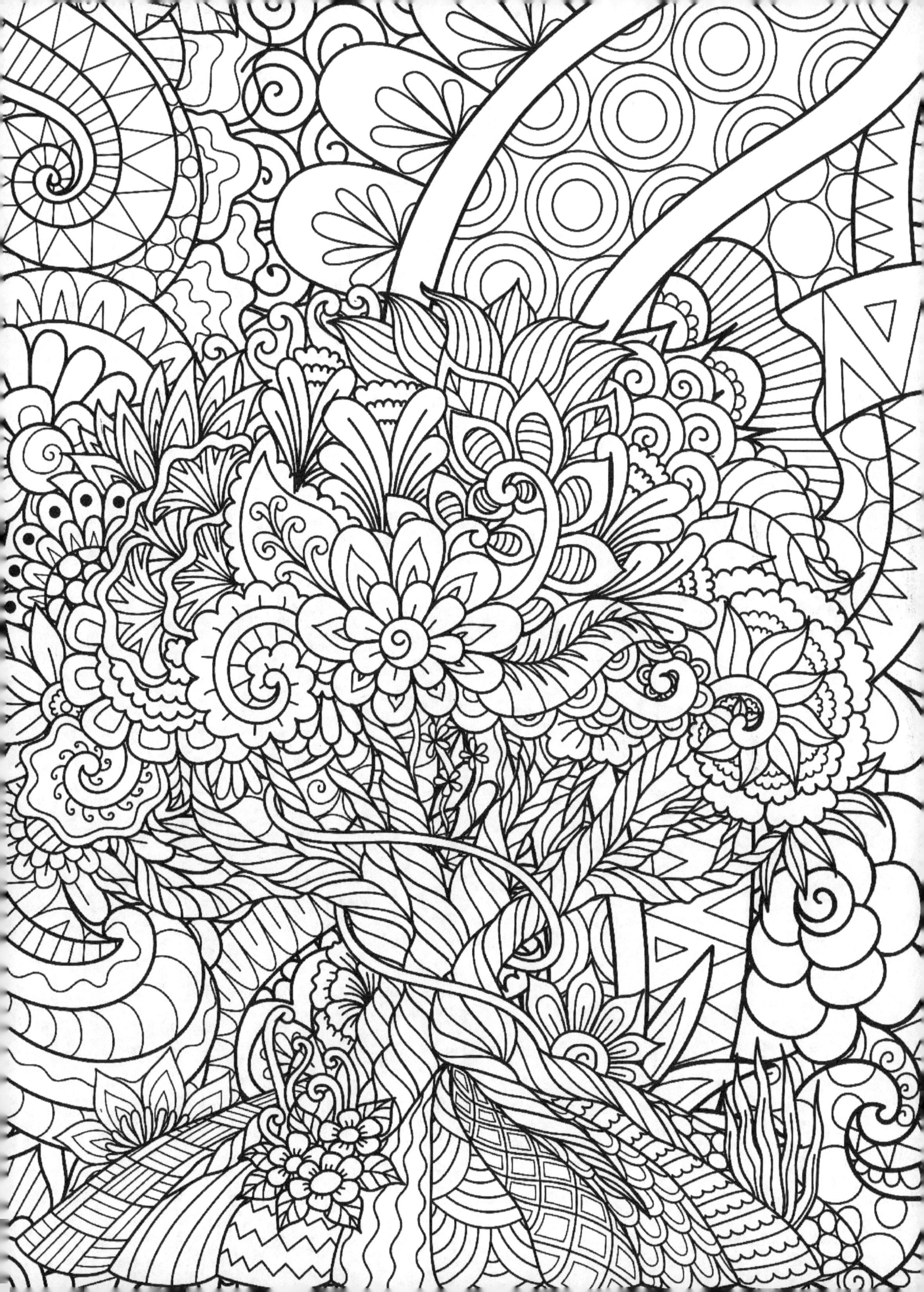

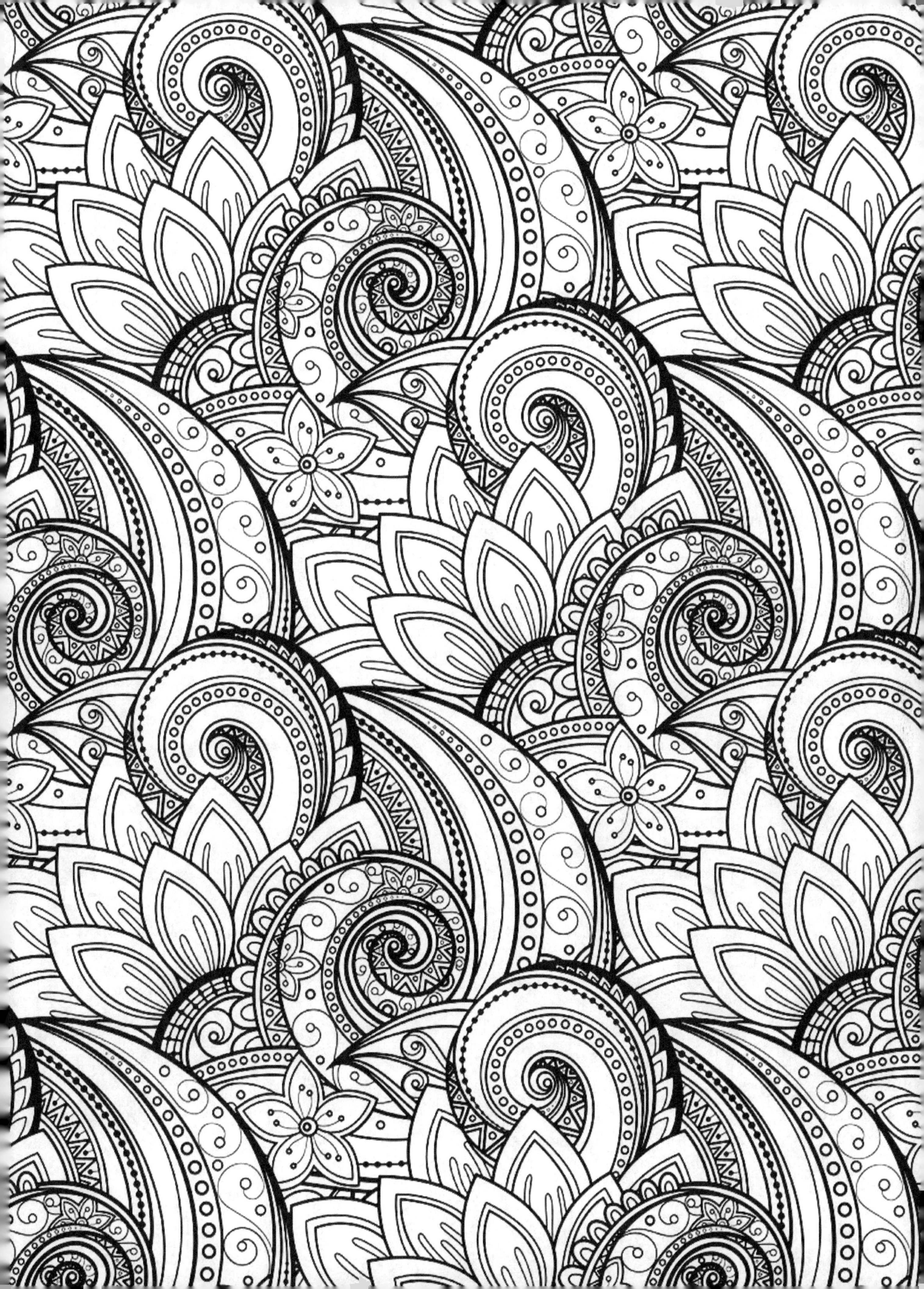

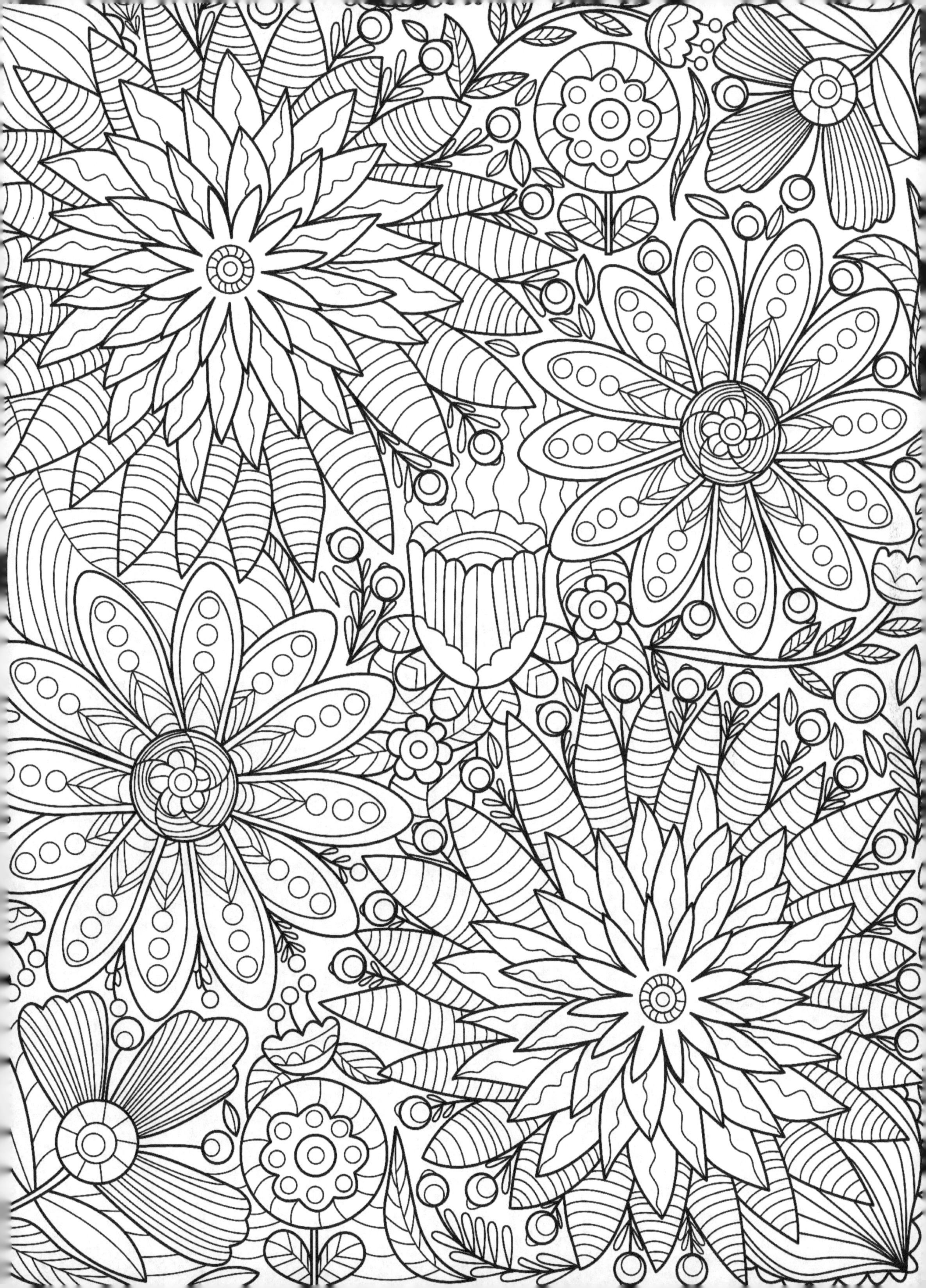

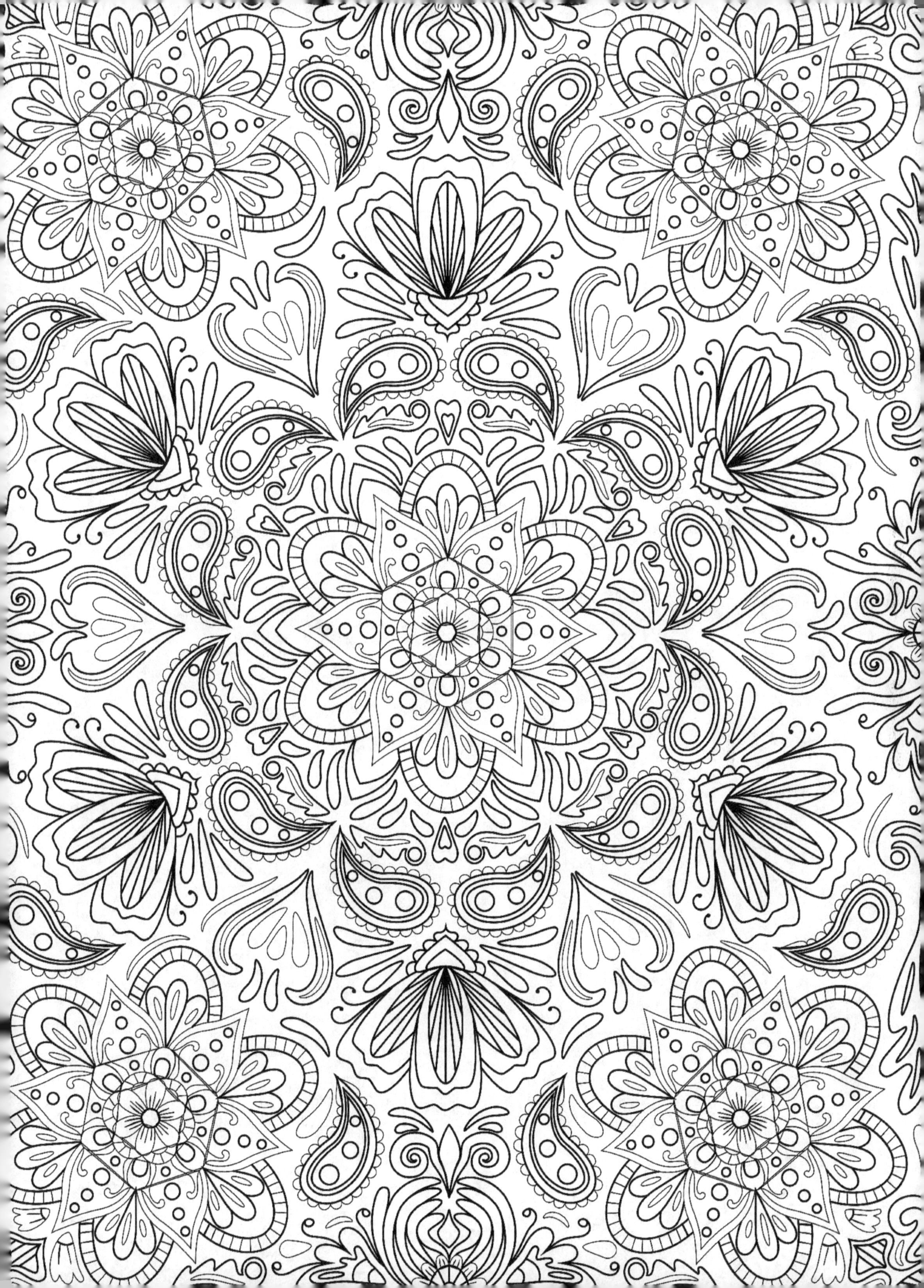

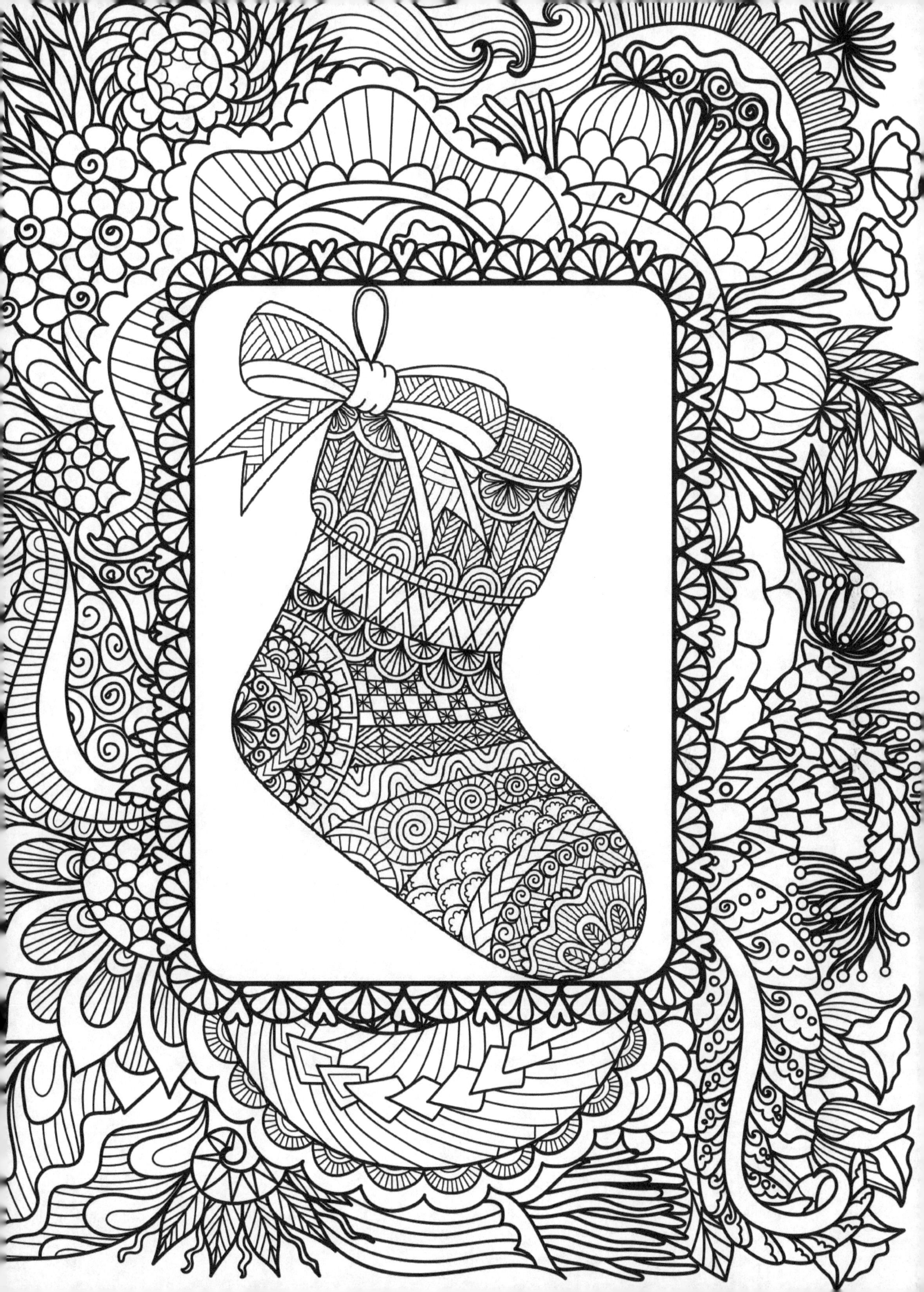

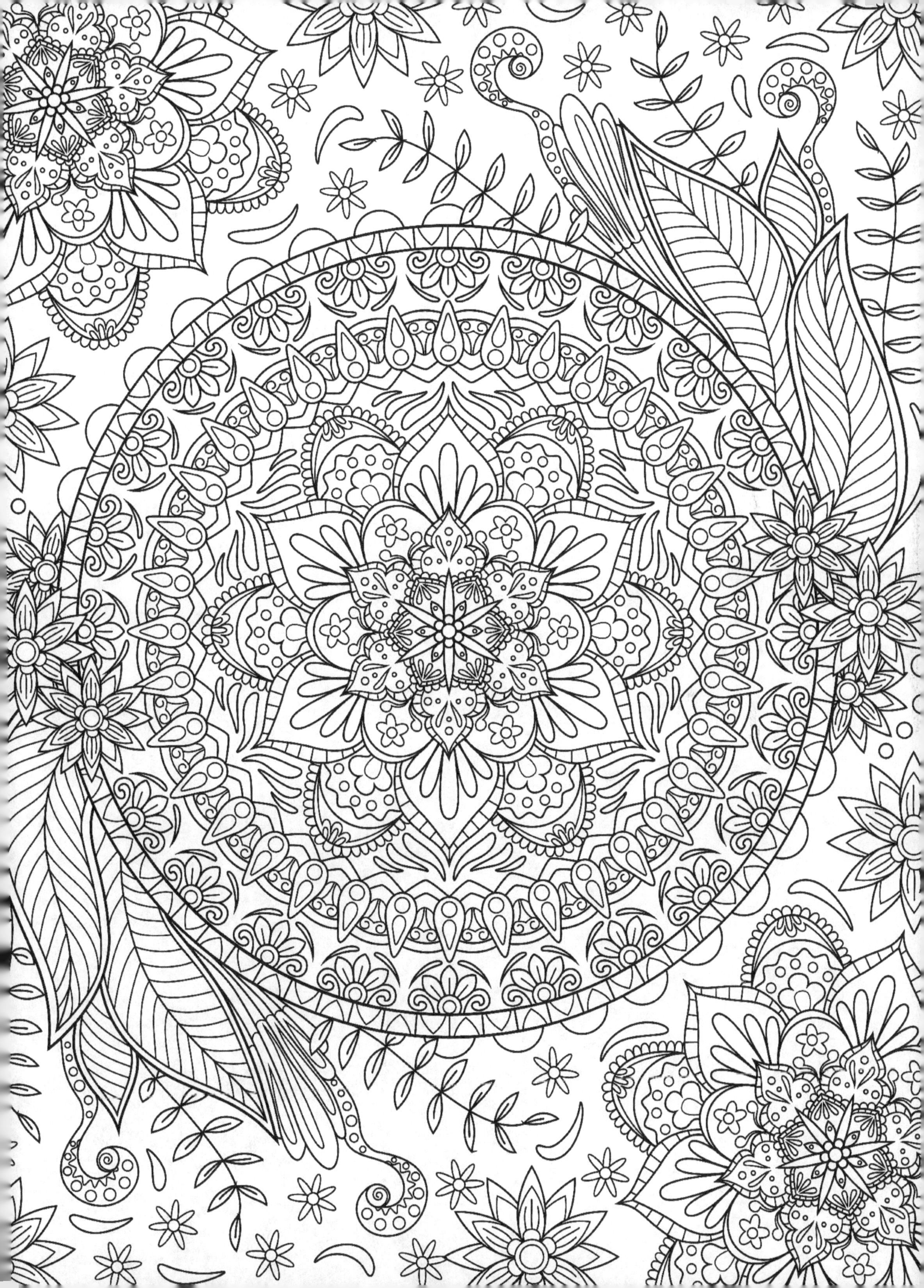

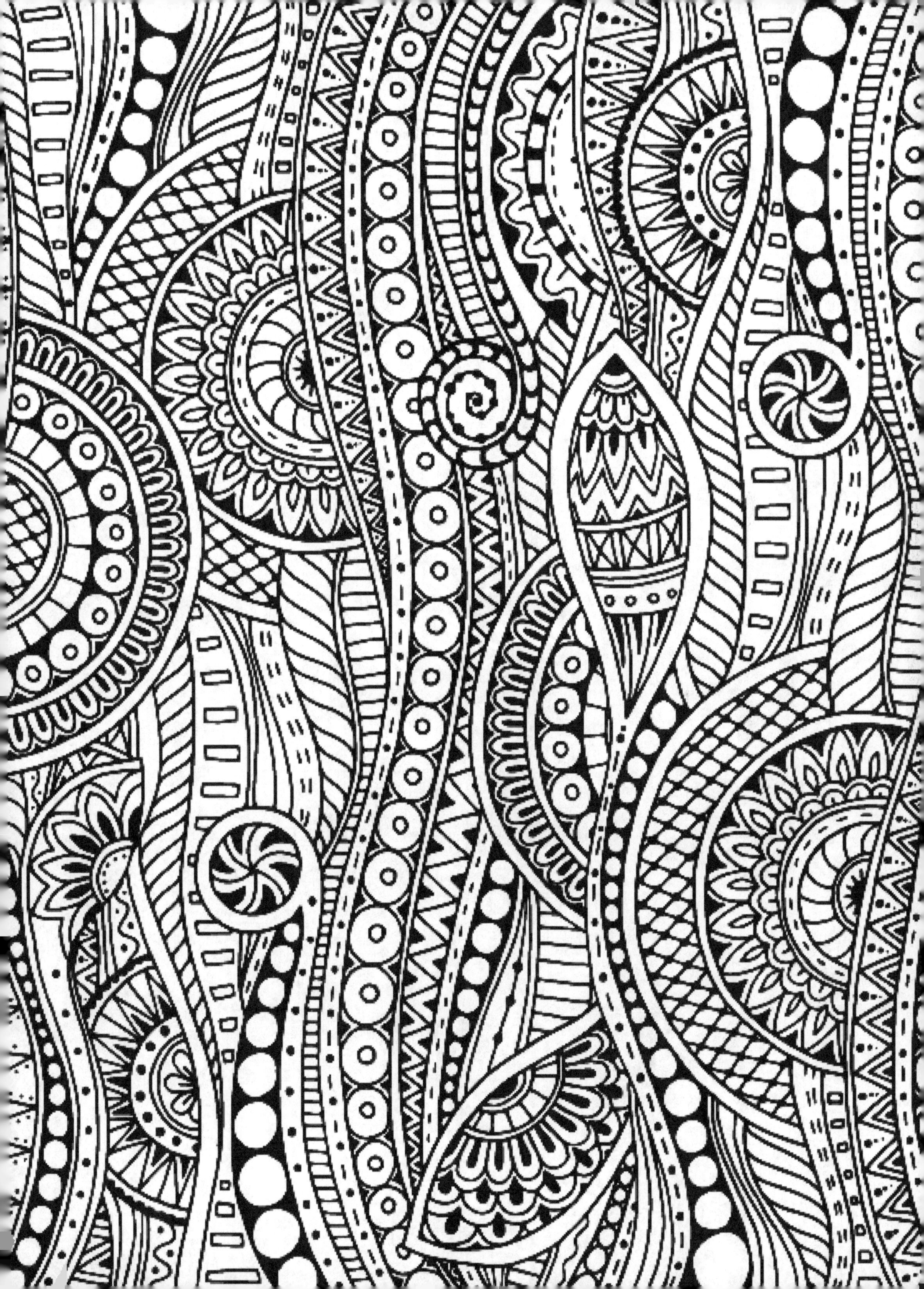

Thank You

Made in United States
Troutdale, OR
08/09/2023

11914814R10064